POETRY RE'

S U M M E R   1 9 9 6   V O L U M E
EDITOR PETER FORBE
PRODUCTION MARTIN DF
SUBSCRIPTIONS AND ADVERTISING

GW00500581

CONTENTS

LONDON MAGAZINE

FICTION * MEMOIRS * CRITICISM * POETRY

CINEMA * ARCHITECTURE * PHOTOGRAPHY

THEATRE * ART * MUSIC

'A fantastic magazine whose place in the history of 20th century literary life grows ever more secure and significant' – *William Boyd, Evening Standard*

Each issue contains over 50 pages of poems and reviews of poetry.

Recent and forthcoming critical essays include:

C. K. Stead on Craig Raine and Thom Gunn

Alan Ross on Derek Walcott and St. Lucia

Marshall Walker on Edwin Morgan

Michael O'Neill on Stephen Spender and Gavin Ewart

Dennis O'Driscoll on Berryman and Yeats

Subscriptions:
£28.50 p.a. (six issues) to 30 Thurloe Place, London SW7

Single copies £5.99 from discriminating bookshops

POETRY REVIEW
SUBSCRIPTIONS
Four issues including postage:

UK individuals £23
Overseas individuals £31
(all overseas delivery is by airmail)
USA individuals $56

Libraries, schools and institutions:
UK £30
Overseas £37
USA $66

Single issue £5.95 + 50p p&p (UK)

Sterling and US dollar payments only. Eurocheques, Visa and Mastercard payments are acceptable.

Bookshop distribution:
Password Books
Telephone 0161 953 4009

Design by Philip Lewis

Typeset by Poetry Review

Printed by Warwick Printing Co Ltd at Theatre Street, Warwick CV34 4DR and at 112 Bermondsey Street, London SE1 3TX
Telephone 0171 378 1579

POETRY REVIEW is the magazine of the Poetry Society. It is published quarterly and issued free to members of the Poetry Society. Poetry Review considers submissions from non-members and members alike. To ensure reply submissions must be accompanied by an SAE or adequate International Reply coupons: Poetry Review accepts no responsibility for contributions that are not reply paid.

Founded 24 February 1909
Charity Commissioners No: 303334
© 1996

THE POETRY SOCIETY

EDITORIAL AND BUSINESS ADDRESS:
22 BETTERTON STREET, LONDON WC2H 9BU

telephone **0171 240 4810**
fax **0171 240 4818**
email **poetrysoc@dial.pipex.com**

ISBN 1 900771 01 2
ISSN 0032 2156

Funded by THE ARTS COUNCIL OF ENGLAND

SERMONS IN STONES

by Peter Forbes

And this our life, exempt from public haunt,
Finds tongues in trees, books in the running brooks,
Sermons in stones, and good in every thing.

(As You Like It)

"ONE MIGHT AS WELL ask how MacNeice's 'notes' can be 'like little fishes'" [in the poem 'Sunday Morning']: Sheenagh Pugh in her letter defending Mark Doty's poetry *(PR,* Vol 86 No 1, p93). Earlier, Pugh talked of the difficulty she had had in explaining to "a rather dull group" how in MacNeice's 'Hold-Up' the "bubbles in the football pools" can "go flat". Pugh's trenchant observations are timely because these days it is not only dull writing groups who raise objections to metaphor and simile. They are assailed by the literal-minded, the politically correct, the postmodernists: all those who no longer believe in the transforming power of art. And yet, a strong case could be made – and I intend to make it – for asserting that such figures of speech are poetry's principal *raison d'être*.

The cause of Sheenagh Pugh's complaint was John Hartley Williams' outburst "how can children smell unopened". Anyone has the right to say that a metaphor doesn't work for them, seems forced and arbitrary: these arguments of course were always levelled against the Metaphysicals, and more recently against the Martians. As Sheenagh Pugh says, if you have to explain the mechanics of a metaphor, it kills the magic. But if tolerance of metaphor is currently rather low – as I believe it is – a certain amount of explanation seems necessary.

A metaphor is a conceptual fusion: two or more ideas, images or entire realms of discourse are conflated in one phrase. It is not generally noticed that metaphor plays a crucial role in our relations with the physical world. Metaphors refer to our emotions, mood, mental states, but their content is resolutely physical. The Pugh/Hartley Williams argument revolves around whether or not candles are a fit metaphor for children. Candles are a familiar enough stage property in poetry, one would have thought ("Out, out, brief candle"). In fact such questions are crucial to the current postmodernist debate about the nature of reality and our knowledge of it. If you cannot describe human emotions without invoking the physical world, notions of alienation and the severance of the signifier from the signified start to look rather forced.

Transports of delight

To convey emotions in language requires a vehicle – what else does the word "convey" suggest? And the word "vehicle" in this sentence simultaneously occupies two realms: it is an object, a piece of technology, and it is also a metaphor. In talking about subjective emotions, I have used an object from the physical world. But aren't these worlds, since Galileo, distinct and unbridgeable? How is it then that, almost without thinking, in trying to describe how writers deal with emotions, a mingling of the objective and subjective has occurred? In MacNeice's 'The Old Story' "the waves behind her / Drubbing the memory up and down the pebbles" combines the emotional and physical drubbing in one economical line.

The vehicle for the emotions is to be found in the physical world. The blunt words for emotions – joy, fear, pain, grief, anxiety, anger, hatred – are themselves null: they do not evoke the emotions they denote. And the most powerful passages of writing – those in which the reader vicariously enjoys or suffers the emotions described – nearly always demonstrate an inter-penetration of the human and the physical world. "To be or not to be" is a riot of such mingling. This is not surprising, as emotions themselves are attended by eruptions of the biological into the human: tears, sexual fluids, adrenaline, visceral sensations.

In all societies, such intrusions of the body into social life are the subject of taboo – the element of transgression has to be acknowledged and ritualised. A familiar example is the "Bless you" sneeze reflex. This is rationalised as a charm against the escape of the soul from the body, thus permitting the devil to fly in, but more fundamentally it is an element of the libidinous natural world breaking the placid social surface that we construct for others. Many people similarly feel the need to 'legitimise' the eruption of orgasm with a verbal spell, but since only private orgasms are permitted, this is uncertain territory.

At the lowest level, I'm reminded of the cartoon

in which an outraged man at the dinner table splut-
ters: "Damnit, man, you've just farted in front of
my wife". "I'm sorry, I didn't know it was her turn",
was the riposte.

In poetry we are concerned not with eruptions
of the physical into the social but with appropria-
tions, by means of words, of bits of physical terrain.
Poets have always, at least implicitly, been animists,
using emotional transference from the animate to
the inanimate, seeing tongues in trees etc. This tech-
nique is sometimes pejoratively called the pathetic
fallacy*, but I don't believe it is a fallacy at all.

When emotion is transferred from the human to
the physical world what happens linguistically is that
an epithet is transferred from one object to another
which, logically, it cannot qualify. In Octavius
Caesar's "If 'twill tie up thy discontented sword" from
Anthony and Cleopatra the discontent belongs to the
holder of the sword not the object itself, but all tools
are extensions of the body and just as we act and even
feel through them, our emotions are expressed
through them also. Such transfers are not restricted
to simple epithets such as "discontented": in
metaphor they become images bound up in phrases.

One of the most perfect metaphors in
Shakespeare is "sleep that knits up the ravelled
sleave of care" from *Macbeth*. In such a metaphor
two things happen simultaneously: we understand
the sense of the statement – sleep that soothes away
the cares of the day – but we also see in our mind's
eye the physical image which has been yoked to that
statement. We see care as a ravelled woollen sleeve,
all its stitching undone, coiling and kinking irre-
deemably. But sleep really can knit up the frayed
and fretted loose ends of the day's worries, so we
see, as in a reverse-action film, the sleeve remaking
itself. It is this stereoscopic vision, the simultaneous
apprehension of the statement and the image,
which creates the intense emotion of pathetic fallac-
ies (or metaphors, for they are interchangeable).
And this vision can only be created by such a
mingling of the human and the physical worlds.

Shakespeare dived in and out of the physical
world with wonderful confidence: "most fond and
winnowed opinions", "cormorant-devouring time",

"trouble deaf heaven with my bootless cries",
"russet yeas and honest kersey noes". We get from
these an intensification of emotion by the surpris-
ing physicality. No one has ever accused
Shakespeare of being mechanical – he is the very
model of earthy wit and soul, but time and again
his epithets and images come from physical trades –
"the cement of our love" (*Anthony and Cleopatra*),
"an unvarnished tale" (*Othello*), "As if the world
should cleave, and that slain men / Should solder
up the rift" (*Anthony and Cleopatra*), "how he glis-
ters through my rust" (*The Winter's Tale*).
Incidentally, "unvarnished" has become so familiar
and varnish such an old-fashioned substance, that
its physicality has been all but lost.

So natural does metaphor seem that even the
extreme case of transferred epithet known as hypal-
lage can often work, as in "He twiddled a thoughtful
steering wheel" (P. G. Wodehouse). This is comic
rather than moving but it is undoubtedly more effec-
tive than "thoughtfully, he twiddled the steering
wheel". I claim that this inter-penetration of the
human and the physical is our natural way of being
in the physical world, and that the physical world is
"organic to the self", giving the lie to the facile notion
of modern man's alienation from nature.

The lounging logo

The most graphic evidence for the efficacy and func-
tionality of emotional transference comes, like so
much else, from contemporary television advertis-
ing. Like poets, advertisers work largely with moods
– and how do you show a mood? In the old days you
simply posed people against suggestive backgrounds,
as in the OXO happy family ads starring Katie. More
recently, there has been a vogue for sultry mini-
dramas suggesting all kinds of passionate intrigue.
But what is more interesting is the eruption of
computer-generated virtual reality into naturalistic
scenes. These animations bring objects alive amongst
people: in a British Rail advert, shoes transmogrify
into carpet slippers which curl up with pleasure and
contentment; the Penguin in the logo on a paper-
back voluptuously lounges in its oval hammock. The
message seems to be that the mood of the contented

---

* The term was coined by Ruskin to denote the false appearance of things "when we are under the influence of emotion
or contemplative fancy". Ruskin finds this debased technique only in second-order poets, curiously ignoring the case of
Shakespeare, whom he admits to the first rank despite his work being awash with pathetic fallacies. In *Modern Painters*
Ruskin wrote extensively on nature and art, sometimes coming close to Hopkins's enquiry into the forms of nature. But
Ruskin was a true Victorian and absolute truth to nature, slavish mimesis, was his great artistic touchstone – a serious limi-
tation on his enterprise.

traveller is best expressed by projecting it onto unusually expressive objects. In a throat medicine advert, the rasp of a sore throat is shown by a bunch of celery in a jug on the table in front of the sufferer suddenly stripping itself into shreds which reconstitute after taking the tablet. In yet another, a mini car bounces spontaneously on the forecourt, blowing out and sucking in its cheeks, doffing its wing mirrors, mimicking the puffing and preening of its proud owner.

All this is so analogous to the poetic process that you can imagine the advertisers sitting down with the *Dictionary of Quotations*, or even a slim volume or two, looking for likely metaphors to illustrate. Take Craig Raine's poem 'Shallots', almost a script for a computer-animated sequence. A languorous garden is conveyed by the conceit of Indian imagery, mostly musical (a cross-senses transference, or synaesthesia, which is one of the key techniques by which the physical world enters our emotions):

We inhale the grass
and listen with our eyes
to the long, slow raga of summer

Words chasing their tails

All this riotous cross-traffic of images, words, and mingled senses represents an insouciant challenge flung in the face of postmodernist prohibitions. For if Shakespeare believed that beyond words lay the world, that words could be a "mirror to nature" the most influential literary critic in the world today, Jacques Derrida, believes that "there is nothing beyond the text" – the connection between words and reality has been severed. To enjoy metaphor fully today we need to clear this hurdle out of the way (not that one can refer to postmodernism and hurdles in the same sentence: there are no hurdles in or beyond the text).

That parenthesis illustrates the problem that for postmodernists cripples language in its dealings with the world: reflexivity. The sentence "To enjoy

metaphor . . ." has embedded in it the problem it is trying to talk about. The postmodernist philosopher Hilary Lawson has said "It is the role of language rather than the role of the subject that threatens to dismantle the edifice of objective reality".

Language does exhibit paradoxes of reflexivity or self-referentiality of which the Cretan Liar is the best-known example, introduced by Epimenides in the 6th Century BC. If the Cretan says: "All Cretans are liars", this statement clearly refers to itself, and thus appears to cancel itself out. Many such paradoxes can be formulated. Lawson tends to tie himself in knots of reflexivity, for example: "Its claims [of his book], including this one, are not intended to be held, they do not attempt to stand".

Lawson has convinced himself that all language behaves like this, that every statement undercuts itself. Furthermore, he says: "Today, because of the irreducibly textual character of all beliefs, all areas of certainty are in question". This is the "problem" of reflexivity that is at the heart of contemporary antirealist and postmodern critiques of science and objective reality. But reflexivity is a pseudo-problem.

Lawson's statement about "the *edifice* [my italics] of objective reality" being destroyed by reflexive language contains the clue to the error that runs through a huge strand of modern philosophy, from Nietzsche, through Wittgenstein, to Heidegger, and Derrida. The key is the word "edifice".

The problem of reflexivity is always stated in the same way. A single statement is made such as "I make no absolute assertions", and instantly we see that the statement is self-contradictory or reflexive. The statement is in the form of a categorical assertion, even as it states that categorical assertions are impossible. But a single statement is not an edifice. Lawson was right to realise the connection between the linguistic problem of representation and the scientific problem of knowledge of the external world. But his analysis is wrong in both domains.

The edifice of language is capable of representation even if certain isolated statements are reflexive. Most possible statements, such as "Move that table over here" are not reflexive (neither does science's claim to representation rest on being able to determine the exact position and momentum of a single particle, but on the vast interlocking skein of chemical relationships and reactions). Propositions and particles disappear up their ani; language and the world are real and grow hand-over-fist by evolutionary niche-creation. It is perfectly possible for a system of representation to be stable even if its elements are not: and this is in fact the case. The familiar stable large-scale world is built of quantum particles that seem to exhibit properties not unlike reflexivity.

Reflexivity emerges when the wrong kind of question is asked. Russell wanted to derive the whole of mathematics from formal logic. Gödel showed that no such closed system was possible. Logical positivism asserted that "only empirically verifiable statements are meaningful", but this premise is not itself empirically verifiable.

Such attempts to limit and constrict, to delve down to an ultimate, self-validating proposition are doomed to failure. To deconstruct the techniques of the currently fashionable philosophers: reflexivity is not a property of language or the world as represented in human consciousness – rather it is a property of the techniques adopted by these philosophers. From Nietzsche, through Heidegger to Derrida, there has been a catastrophic narrowing, an implosion, until a man is left poring over texts, forcing them to contradict themselves, etymologically interrogating every word, convinced that "there is nothing beyond the text". Hilary Lawson says: "However hard one tries to squeeze out reflexive problems, they seem to reappear . . . *Ironically* [my italics], it is in the most rigorous texts that this is most obvious". *Au contraire*, it is the rigour that creates the reflexivity; this kind of rigour is self-defeating. As Aristotle said in the *Nicomachian Ethics*:

> It is the mark of an educated mind to rest satisfied with the degree of precision that the nature of the subject admits, and not to seek exactness when only an approximation is possible.

It might be thought that some of the techniques I have been discussing – visual punning, emotional transference, animation – might owe something to the more playful postmodernists, but the foregoing highlights their crucial difference: visual punning and bootstrapping are centrifugal, expansive generators of new layers of complexity, in contrast to the spirally implosive nature of deconstruction. The philosopher can find no reason for there to be anything, he even finds the question, "why should there be something rather than nothing?" ultimately reflexive (because it already posits the something that might or might not exist); but the evolutionary biologist, the poet, the software writer, revel in the constant creation of new things. Keeping abreast of the tide of possibility is the problem, not pondering the ultimate lack of necessity for the existence of something rather than nothing.

The malapropisms of Fiery Fred

Freud said that he had only rediscovered what every wet nurse knew. Vernacular discourse knows more about representation than the postmodernist theorists. Everyday language has always been naturally metaphoric. "Now we know where the shoe pinches", "He was on his high horse", "mutton dressed as lamb", to have "two strings to one's bow", "if the cap fits", "a fair crack of the whip". If these weren't clichés they would be poetry, and indeed, as Louis MacNeice pointed out, even as clichés they are poetry. Poetic metaphor as a bridge between human beings and the natural world is deeply rooted in pre-literacy. The great fast bowler Freddie Trueman was once quoted by a journalist on the origins of his nickname. Trueman said that they called him 'Fiery' because "it rhymes with Fred". The journalist invited our sniggers but another response is possible. Trueman was demonstrating both his illiteracy and his naive enthusiasm for poetry. Alliteration is an inherently demotic art even if the word itself is unknown to the uneducated. Sportsmen and women are always 'Gorgeous Gussie', 'Fiery Fred', or 'Typhoon Tyson' because finding likenesses in which the sound matches the sense is as instinctive a human activity as breathing.

The delightful world of cliché and refrain

Cliché is a crucial terrain for investigating the relationship of language to the physical world. On one level, the realm of cliché is the scrapyard of metaphor. Clichés are phrases that once embodied the physical world, but which now function only as linguistic counters. As we saw with "the ravelled sleave of care", a live metaphor works because we apprehend both its literal, physical meaning and its meaning-by-analogy at the same time. "A red letter day", "a busted flush", "a dead duck", "an early bird", " a high flier", were all once things, but their thinginess has totally disappeared. People often commit malapropisms with clichés because they have forgotten their literal meaning, for example: "no holes barred" for "no holds barred".

Despite their loss of physicality and metaphorical resonance, no one should despise clichés. The fact that they are recognised by most people who speak the same language is an inestimable aid to communication. And clichés are minor sacraments, enshrining typical cases of human behaviour. We meet them as old friends. Louis MacNeice celebrated their sacramental nature in 'Homage to Clichés' – we should value them because:

Somewhere behind us stands a man, a counter
A timekeeper with a watch and pistol
Ready to shoot and with his shot destroy
This whole delightful world of cliché and refrain –
What will you have my dear? The same again?

But clichés can also be revived, by reasserting their physicality. I am indebted to Craig Raine for demonstrating Dickens' extensive use of such a procedure. Dickens' device is so powerful, it really should be a recognised literary figure with a proper name, but so far it hasn't acquired one. What Dickens does is not to utter the cliché at all, but to illustrate it in an elaborated fantasy or conceit. Take this passage from *Little Dorrit*, cited by Raine:

Everything in Marseilles, and about Marseilles, had stared at the fervid sky, and had been stared at in return, until a staring habit had become universal there. Strangers were stared out of countenance by staring white houses, staring white walls, staring white streets, staring tracts of arid roadstaring hills from which verdure was burnt away.

The phrase behind this is *the glare of the sun*. This is doubly interesting for our purpose because: 1) the passage is blatantly animistic, it is a pathetic fallacy; 2) the cliché is actually a pun – glare can refer equally well to an optical effect or to a penetrating look. It is a word with animism inbuilt: it refers equally to the thing perceived and the perceiving organ. Other clichés revived by Dickens in this fashion are "coming down in the world", "warm as toast", "living in the past", but he did not invent the technique. It began, of course, like everything else, with

Shakespeare. When Macbeth says: "The wine of life is drawn, and the mere lees / Is left this vault to brag of" he is *scraping the bottom of the barrel*.

Shakespeare's techniques are as available and valid today as they were then. John Fuller's 'Her Morning Dreams' has the lines:

Its hopes on threads, its memories in pockets,
The sluggish mouth disowning all its streams.

Books in the running brooks.

Double Exposure

GWYNETH LEWIS ON "THE ANIMATION OF THE LITERARY WORLD" – METAPHOR

IF SIMILE IS a conventional weapon, then metaphor is a nuclear device. In school, in lessons on figurative language, we were taught that a metaphor is always introduced by "is", a simile by "as" or "like". We identified such images as if they were a rare form of exotic life in a text. They called out in our set books, sporting unlikely plumage. We caged them with pencil marks. However, this schoolgirl definition of metaphor is like describing Armageddon as a firework display. Metaphor's a time bomb, you can hear it tick.

I only began to understand the power of metaphor a few years ago, when I realised that poetry is the animation of the literary world. Good cartoon art does use simile but it always resorts to metaphor for its punchlines. In *Tom and Jerry* a simile would be Tom, the cat, imagining a desirable future for himself, described in a thought bubble, well out of reality. To see the metaphor, think of a Tom who's just stunned himself with a garden rake in his wild chase after Jerry. Not only are the lights on and nobody home, his eyelids have become blinds pulled down over the windows of his eyes. Tom isn't *like* a deserted house, his body *is* that shell. In this case the stylistic answer to violence is metaphor. Simile simply wouldn't jar the nerves in the same way.

One of the greatest joys of poetry is that it is, like cartoons, freed from the laws of physics. The poet/ cartoonist's main tool in this job is metaphor. Imagine a cartoon fight scene in a kitchen. A weak man is thrown back against a radiator. He turns into a tea towel, slides down to the floor where he's reconstituted as a man. A simile would have told us that the man felt as weak as a dishcloth. The metaphor makes us wince because it goes further, making a human body share in the sickening limpness of a rag. Only the animator's art can give the stunned man his bones again and make him walk.

Being freed from the normal laws of time and space doesn't mean that metaphor can be merely fanciful. It has to be accurate. The complex mathematical ratios set up by a good metaphor have to *compute* or they become nothing more than distracting verbiage. To take a straightforward example:

The heron is a Presbyterian minister
Standing gloomy in his long grey coat

Looking at his own reflection in a Sabbath loch.

Every now and again, pronouncing fire and brimstone
He snatches at an unsuspecting trout
And stands with a lump in his throat.

The congregation of midges laughs at him in Gaelic.
He only prays for them, head bent into grey rain
As a lark sings psalms half a mile above.

This poem by Kenneth C. Steven was published, with a photograph of the bird, in the RSPB magazine *Birds* in 1994. The photograph proved the minister/ heron comparison to be perceptive. The ratios work out neatly: heron is to minister as trout is to his words, as midges are to congregation. Setting up a series of parallel equivalents may be enjoyable for a while, but successful metaphor always goes one step further, beyond these one-to-one matches. The last stanza introduces the cultural tensions between an English-speaking minister and his Gaelic-speaking congregation. Compared to the flying lark with its psalms, the heron is a clumsy intercessor between God and his creatures, caught up in political difficulties of which the lark is free. This startling and subtle new perspective is only possible in the poem because the initial physical comparison on which the metaphor is based is solid.

Metaphor is a form of double exposure. In the example above the two images – heron and minister – are as if printed on two pieces of material of equal transparency, so that both images can be seen clearly at the same time. Of course, the poet needs to keep strict control of the balance of power between the two images. I've dumped more poems than I care to admit where the metaphor ran away with me, blotting out the original object of description. Rainer Maria Rilke's poem 'Spanish Dancer' is a wonderful example of masterly poetic control of metaphor. The central conceit of the poem is that flamenco dance is, in some way, a fire surrounding the dancer as she moves. So closely are the two terms developed that the dancer in the poem herself seems to catch fire:

One upward glance and she ignites her hair
and, whirling faster and faster, fans her dress
into passionate flames, till it becomes a furnace

from which, like startled rattlesnakes, the long naked arms uncoil, aroused and clicking.

So confident is Rilke of his metaphor here that he can introduce a subordinate snake simile without tearing the fabric of the image. The base image needs to be sufficiently pronounced that we don't lose the terms of the initial comparison, but not so rigid that the fluidity of transformation is denied to us. It's like developing the kind of vision which can see the sky reflected on the surface of a pool at the same time as observing the fish nibbling at the weeds under the surface. The great poets not only see both things simultaneously, they can also watch a dog ruining it all by running through the water. As we saw with the heron/minister example, good metaphor doesn't just rely on two terms, it magically introduces a third which shouldn't, by strict logic, be there at all.

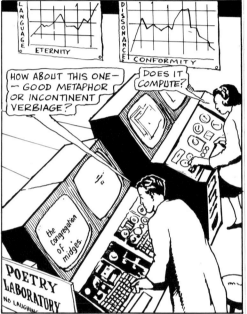

Similes create a universe parallel to the one under consideration. When Milton describes Satan jumping into the Garden of Eden in an epic simile he takes the reader away from the main poetic path into a suggestive side route:

> As when a prowling wolf,
> Whom hunger drives to seek new haunt for prey,
> Watching where shepherds pen their flocks at eve
> In hurdl'd cotes amid the field secure,
> Leaps o'er the fence with ease into the fold:
> Or as a thief bent to unhoard the cash
> Of some rich burgher, whose substantial doors,
> Cross-barr'd and bolted fast, fear no assault,
> In at the window climbs, or o'er the tiles;
> So clomb this first grand thief into God's fold.
> (*Paradise Lost*, IV, 11. 183-93)

Metaphor's the tool of the poetic terrorist who's not interested in diversions, however instructive, but in identifications. Metaphor actually folds the fabric of the world in order to place two objects on top of each other. The result is a kind of epistemological tuck in the surface of reality. What metaphor does is show how things that appear widely different are, viewed in a certain way, essentially similar. In this the deployer of metaphor is far from being a fantasist, he has insight into some basic truths. Scientists have already drawn our attention to the way in which the world's made up of a number of basic shapes. It appears to be no accident that the outlines of a delta, a fork of lightning, veins in a body or the branches of a tree all share the same outline. So, when I write that "trees stand delta to the sky" I'm not being fanciful or poetic, but simply literal. Metaphor is just one more way of describing the world literally. It has been said that poetry makes use of science's discarded metaphors. This is not to say that poetry uses disproved theories, but that in its thirst for new models to describe the world, poetry grabs the language most recently formed in the lab. Like any pioneering research, such information is quickly superseded by new developments in understanding, so such metaphors are usually provisional.

The world described by metaphor is post-apocalyptic. It's a literal description of a world stripped of the dimensions of time, or space, or both. Metaphor struggles out at the frontier between language and eternity, it points to an order in the process of being formed in the poet's sensibility. It's a circle of covered wagons shooting at the Apaches of time and the cavalry's going to be a long while coming. One of the reasons why poetry is such an enduring art form is that, more than any other, save music, it's able to tinker with the dominance of time over our lives. Metre, as Joseph Brodsky said, is reconstructed time. Rhyme is an ordering of difference within the rhythm of a language's internal echoes. Far from being a discrete figurative ornament, metaphor is even more deeply implicated in this restructuring of time. By drawing out the deep puns in the world – between deltas and trees, for example

– metaphor is the substantial rhyme of poetry, of which the chiming of end-rhymes is but an audible equivalent. These deep echoes within reality are recognised at the peril of the time and space in between them, which is why time may literally be said to worship language.

This can go even further metaphysically. In his sonnet 'Prayer' George Herbert uses a whole string of metaphors to describe his subject:

> Prayer the Churches banquet, Angels age,
>   Gods breath in man returning to his birth,
>   The soul in paraphrase, heart in pilgrimage,
> The Christian plummet sounding heav'n and earth.

The cumulative effect of this list of often surprising images – with prayer, among other things, described as "the milkie way" and "the bird of paradise" – is to give us a sense that Herbert is playing on the harmonic tones of language, trying to convey something that's beyond even the metaphorical. He may even be suggesting that the only way we can begin to understand God is to think of Him as a collection of metaphors more diverse than the human mind can comprehend at one time. The metaphor points beyond itself towards omniscience.

If metaphor is the deep rhyme of poetry then part of the skill in using it involves bringing out the difference, as well as the similarities, between the two terms being merged. In Welsh-language prosody a line can be rejected metrically because it has "bai rhy debyg", that is, the fault of being aurally too similar to its predecessor. Conformity is barren, dissonance fruitful. Robert Frost wrote that all metaphors are imperfect and that this is the source of their beauty. This is also the source of their subversiveness. By making unlikely alliances between vastly different objects and freeing them from the space and time which divides them, metaphor totally undermines the importance of both dimensions. It's no accident that Shakespeare turns to metaphor when trying to describe the ultimate relationship between love and time – "Love's not Time's fool" – because love, like metaphor (which is a form of attentive love), can survive chronology, even while it seems to exist only at its mercy.

The prophecy of Isaiah shows how this mechanism works. When Isaiah says that "the wolf and the lamb will feed together", what seems to be an absurd and impossible situation – according to what we know of the habits of wolves and their tendency to eat lambs – becomes a stunning vision of redemption if you imagine an order of grace in which the gentleness of a lamb and the ferocity of a wolf are of equal value and, therefore, at peace with each other. Thus, Isaiah's animals are metaphorical in our own, fallen order, but will be together literally in the new world to which the prophet is committed.

There is, of course, a political agenda to this. There should be a Government Health Warning against metaphor because of its iconoclastic relationship with the status quo. Its most radical aspect is the poet's commitment not to a promised future or a glorious past, but to a tense which can be called the eternal present. This tense, with its implicit trust in the individual's vision above all other kinds of logic – temporal or physical – offers no purchase to politicians or other manipulators of mind. It is in this sense that poets, as Yehuda Amichai has argued, are able to inoculate the rest of society against evil. This is how Dylan Thomas can write in 'Poem on His Birthday' –

> Dark is a way and light is a place,
>   Heaven that never was
> Nor will be ever is always true

– suggesting that even if you're not religious the re-ordering of time offered by metaphor exists, whether you want it to or not.

There is, however, a price to pay for seeing an order of reality which is usually invisible to others. In Vladimir Nabokov's fascinating novel *Transparent Things*, the author chronicles four visits made by the main character to one hotel in Switzerland and draws out the parallels between them, almost by placing one on top of another, through the main character's memory. Nabokov shows that he also had no illusions about the fact that the surface of everyday life is deceptive:

> A thin veneer of immediate reality is spread over
> natural and artificial matter, and whoever wishes to
> remain in the now, with the now, on the now,
> should please not break its tension film. Otherwise
> the inexperienced miracle-worker will find himself
> no longer walking on water but descending upright
> among staring fish.

For who's to say that the literal film of things is more real than that which poets see by means of the metaphors they use to describe it? Especially if those visions overlap and confirm each other within a generation, across a tradition? For what is tradition except a way in which poets move in the slipstreams of each other's work for no other reason than to cheat the time that divides them?

Lyrical Scraps

by Edna Longley

CRAIG RAINE

Clay: Whereabouts Unknown

Penguin Books, £7.99,
ISBN 0 14 058767 5

CRAIG RAINE TELLS US that *Clay: Whereabouts Unknown* contains poems "written in the decade" when he produced *History: The Home Movie*. This suggests that he regards his new (slim) volume as lyrical scraps from an epic feast. Raine's epic, however, I found indigestible and possibly undigested: a misuse of literary gifts which incline more to image and subjectivity than to narrative or reportage. Happily, a number of poems here recover the intensity diminished by his ambition to fill a large canvas. At the same time, the contrast between the two collections, together with some continuing structural problems, raises wider questions about the metaphysics of genre and form.

Craig Raine is an extremely talented writer who has never quite found the medium that would develop his vision, the vision that would develop his medium. One still has a sense of material which has been processed without being modified by form in a deeper sense. He draws on a stock of ingenuities ("the poached egg like an octopus", "the turban in a tangerine", "a cricket ball like Saturn") that do not really belong more to one poem than another.

This is probably why I liked 'Perfume', 'Redmond's Hare', and 'Heaven on Earth': all poems that explore their earthly force-fields with minimal interference from Raine's "Martian" reflex. 'Perfume' lightly, tantalisingly evokes desire for a woman in terms of where and how her perfume might be applied: "a naked wrist, / another wrist, / / caressing each other / like delicate lovers…" Raine's obsession with the body and his visual erotics figure

more robustly in 'Redmond's Hare', a poem which proceeds as voyeuristic necrophilia until the speaker "look[s] out the sex" and realises his human and literary presumption:

> female, a little black-eye,
> too tender to touch,
> which only looked at me
> and I was crushed…

'Heaven on Earth' creates a domestic cosmos which embraces and transforms all its constituents from "the wren at her millinery" to fetching in the washing: "and everything you hold, / two floating shirts, a sheet, / ignores the law of gravity…" Here Raine's images move beyond simile into metaphor. When they do not, as in 'A Chest of Drawers' from the sequence 'The Prophetic Book', his impulse becomes atomised and centrifugal. Although this elegy for Seamus Heaney's mother ends with a powerful impression of death ("the long look we lived in / fixed at last on a chest of drawers"), other effects show Raine's roving eye at its random worst:

> Out of oblivion, this,
> philosophers, fandango dancers,
> a Russian-speaking budgerigar,
> the torch inside a television,
> form and refusal of form,
> the thalidomide seal, God,
> and the perspex shrimp.

The glib opposition – and perhaps alibi –"form and refusal of form" gives the game away. The catalogue as exploited by Hopkins or MacNeice is not a list but a syntax, even when it calls attention to the variety/incongruity of phenomena and of language. Raine's "turban in a tangerine" is a detachable iconic item in 'The Prophetic Book''s listing of "the world / that is taken for granted". But when MacNeice in 'Snow' "peels and portions a tangerine", he moves beyond appearances to complex structures that are meshed with the structure of the poem itself. It is, in fact, Raine's imagination that does not fully enter the world of differences, a world incorrigibly plural. To define the horizons of a poem need not mean falsely imposing closure, order or transcendence. It does mean exercising judgement as to what makes this poem distinctive and necessary. I have long thought that Raine's sensory receptivity has something in common with MacNeice's. This being so, he might think about why *Autumn Journal* succeeds and *Autumn Sequel* largely fails.

Rhythm, of course, is crucial to the act of artistic selection. In *History: The Home Movie* Raine employs a monotonous and fussy three-line stanza which allows insufficient room for the rhetorical and dramatic manoeuvres, the play between voice(s) and stanza, that his subject-matter might seem to require. In *Clay: Whereabouts Unknown* he widens his technical range again: couplets, quatrains, seven-line stanzas, free verse, occasional rhyme, a successful prose poem. If this is deliberate rather than miscellaneous, it will be interesting to see how he reconciles the rhythmical tendencies represented by gapped modernist lines on the one hand, and, on the other, over-insistent refrains like that of 'A Chest of Drawers': "Out of oblivion, birds", "Out of oblivion, this", "Out of oblivion, dogs..."

"Out of oblivion" is over-insistent partly because it seeks to impose philosophical order – a vague universality – on the poem's catalogues. The stanza quoted above not only breaks up into phrases but bewilders feeling; are we meant to ponder "thalidomide" as tragedy, or to conjure up seals and admire the visual conceit? It might be said that an elegy properly evokes life, death, mutilation. Raine, however, depends too often on shallow contrasts: the miraculous "world / that is taken for granted", the "world [as] a beautiful woman", versus a generalised *lacrimae rerum*. He sums up 'The Prophetic Book' as a poem "of sustained wonder at the world – its limitless, offhand beatitudes, its mysteries and its bleak brevities".

This implies that a kind of omni-poem might get everything in without "bleak brevities" causing too much strain. Just as *History: The Home Movie* lacked a historical grasp of the present to chasten and focus its version of the past, so Raine's elegies, the central mode of this volume, can appear hasty or intrusive. Despite their "I" and "you", the voice's subjectivity does not always split to dramatise the meaning of a particular life and death. His concern with the decay of the body ("Liver-coloured lips / await us in the mirror, / glands will cobble our armpits") once again seems undifferentiated. We cannot doubt his anguish over "dead beloved bodies", the notable tenderness of his sensibility. Yet it is metaphor and metaphysics, allied to emotional precision, that make any verse-fettered grief both particular and universal. Raine's elegy for Hans Keller begins: "There will be more of this..." But if his poetry is to keep pace with mortality, it will need to vary its challenges more cunningly.

JOHN GREENING

TO JOHANNES GUTENBERG

You taught us how the world could be contained
Between stiff boards, reduced to type, to a row
Of lead: preserved, passed on by mirror-code
To any future, even this, where multi-laned
Our information runs its rings, hare-brained,
And wails and mocks the passing of the slow
Cold dawn of print on page. Books will still grow
As grapes are red. But look – this untrained
Circuitry is cocooning us: no need
For labour here, the hourly vintage plays
Direct from every lap, its icons bubble
A character from light with lightning speed
And disregard for all you hauled, screwed, pressed
Out of the dark – yes, and thought immovable.

Something Rank and Strange

SOME OF ELIOT'S POEMS OF 1920 REPRESENT THE SUMP OF METAPHOR. PAUL BAILEY
ASSESSES ANTHONY JULIUS'S CHASTENING STUDY OF A CORRUPTED SENSIBILITY

ANTHONY JULIUS
T. S. Eliot, anti-Semitism and literary form
Cambridge University Press, £30,
ISBN 0 521 47063 3

ANTHONY JULIUS'S DENSELY ARGUED and thoughtful book was published in the autumn of 1995, when it was largely unnoticed in the literary pages of the national newspapers. John Gross reviewed it favourably in the *Sunday Telegraph*, and that was about the extent of the critical attention it received. Then, earlier this year, Tom Paulin rescued it from obscurity by using it as the basis for a reassessment of T. S. Eliot's writings and reputation which was published in the *London Review of Books* under the title 'Undesirable'. Paulin's article ends with a confident prediction: "For all its impressive scholarly detail, Julius's study is only the beginning of a long process of revisionist criticism which should diminish the overwhelming, the stifling cultural authority which Eliot's *oeuvre* has acquired".

It is Paulin's view that there exists a "malignity" in Eliot's art. He finds it "terrifying": "It's so firm and so quiet, because like a true politician Eliot never apologises and he never explains". In *T. S. Eliot, anti-Semitism, and literary form*, Anthony Julius differentiates painstakingly between Eliot's more subtle brand of anti-Semitism ("firm", perhaps, and relatively "quiet") and that of his friend and mentor Ezra Pound, which was "overt, deep, and practical". Eliot's anti-Semitism is mostly confined to, and contained within, a few poems, dating from 1917 to 1922. These are 'Gerontion', 'Burbank', 'A Cooking Egg' and 'Sweeney Among the Nightingales' from his second collection, *Ara Vos Prec* of 1920, and 'Dirge', which was deleted from *The Waste Land* on the advice of Ezra Pound, for reasons more to do with aestheticism than the nastiness of the sentiments expressed:

Full fathom five your Bleistein lies
Under the flatfish and the squids.
Graves' Disease in a dead jew's eyes!
When the crabs have eat the lids.
Lower than the wharf rats dive

Though he suffer a sea-change
Still expensive rich and strange.

Ariel's song in *The Tempest* is merciful, since its intention is to comfort the anguished Ferdinand, but Eliot's variation on it is entirely without mercy – it gloats at the very spectacle it presents. 'Dirge' was not published in the poet's lifetime, and only emerged in 1971, in *The Waste Land: A Facsimile and Transcript of the Original Drafts Including the Annotations of Ezra Pound*, which was edited by Eliot's widow, Valerie. Alongside 'Dirge' Pound wrote two question marks above the solitary word "doubtful", which bears out what Julius suggests – that it wasn't the anti-Semitism that bothered him.

Whoever made the final decision, it was wise of Eliot or Pound to suppress this squib. The other poems Julius analyses at length have been in print for over seventy years. Generations of critics have defended the lines from 'Gerontion' –

My house is a decayed house,
And the jew squats on the window sill, the owner,
Spawned in some estaminet of Antwerp,
Blistered in Brussels, patched and peeled in London

– by noting that these are the old man's thoughts, not Eliot's. Had Eliot reserved the notion of the squatting lower-case Jew, who was "spawned" and not "born" like a Christian, to this single elder, the defence would be stronger. But the Jew reappears, in 'Burbank with a Baedeker: Bleistein with a Cigar', in which the still-living Bleistein is described thus:

A saggy bending of the knees
And elbows, with the palms turned out,
Chicago Semite Viennese

which "places" him squarely if not fairly in Vienna and Chicago rather than Antwerp and London. Later in the poem come the most notorious, and most offensive, lines –

The rats are underneath the piles.
The jew is underneath the lot

– which Craig Raine, in a review of Julius's book for the *Financial Times*, attributes to the American tourist Burbank, whose "anti-Semitism is a public posture produced by a private derangement". But is it clear, as it is to Raine, that when the lines quoted above are framed by the fragments "On the Rialto once" and "Money in furs. The boatman smiles" they "indicate interior monologue"? Perhaps we should ask, as Julius often does by implication, why Eliot was so partial to *impersonating* anti-Semites.

The minor controversy sparked off by Tom Paulin's article has brought forth one important revelation. In a letter to the *TLS* of May 31, Valerie Eliot discloses that the review of *The Yellow Spot: The Outlawing of Half a Million Human Beings, a collection of facts and documents relating to three years' persecution of German Jews*, which appeared in *The Criterion* of July 1936, was written by Montgomery Belgion, and not by Eliot, as Julius, Paulin, and others have claimed or assumed. In *T. S. Eliot and Prejudice*, published by Faber in 1988, Christopher Ricks suggests that Eliot might have penned it. It seems odd that Mrs Eliot, with her close connection to her husband's publishing house, did not refute Ricks's suggestion at the time, thus preventing much subsequent speculation. Belgion's review, commissioned by Eliot, is a seedy, nit-picking affair. It begins: "There should be somebody to point out that this book, although enjoying a cathedratic blessing" – from the then Bishop of Durham – "is an attempt to rouse moral indignation and sensationalism". The book, in fact, contained incontrovertible evidence about the treatment of Jews in concentration camps, as well as photographs showing anti-Semitic posters and cartoons. Eliot, as editor of *The Criterion*, must have made the decision that *The Yellow Spot* merited a review, and while we are all aware that editors do not always endorse the opinions of their contributors they nevertheless have the power, or moral duty in this instance, to wield the blue pencil. Belgion's article, reproduced in full by Anthony Julius, probably had Eliot's blessing.

It could be said that this book, which began as a Ph.D. thesis, is overlong and often repetitive. And Julius occasionally departs too liberally from Eliot's actual texts, reading hidden meanings into them via his formidable knowledge of the history of anti-Semitism. It is an exaggeration to declare, as he does, that the old man in 'Gerontion' spits out the offending remarks about the Jewish landlord. There is no evidence for this assertion. I think, also, that he is too cavalier on the subject of English anti-Semitism. It definitely was "in the air" in my own childhood and adolescence, and it was frequently voiced by men and women in every respect decent and kindly, save for this one despicable aberration. As late as the 1950s, it was common to hear terms such as "Jew-boy" openly spoken, along with "Some of my best friends are Jews". That Eliot did not move out of this polluted atmosphere and breathe a finer air is a cause for dismay, given his rare sensibility and erudition. There is a snobbishness aligned to Eliot's anti-Semitism of a peculiarly English variety, which was "in the air" until quite recently.

Anthony Julius has been accused of self-righteousness, and the accusation is unfair. His study is informed by respect and admiration. He never forgets that he is concerned with a great talent. And it is precisely because Eliot is a great talent, and not a second-rate versifier and novelist like the much more overtly anti-Semitic Hilaire Belloc, that Julius has been bothered to take him to task. Unlike that vulgar genius Louis-Ferdinand Celine and the Nazi sympathiser, Knut Hamsun, Eliot was a veritable pillar of the Establishment at the end of his life.

When Tom Paulin writes of Eliot's "malignity", he seems to me to be disregarding a necessary source of Young Possum's startling poetic imagination. The "malignity" of the early poems is at one with the eye for squalor in 'Preludes' and the ear for the tortured cadences of desolation. He was fired by a grudge against life. The author of *Four Quartets* and those awful West End plays – replete with what Kenneth Tynan called "well-bred dread" – has no real, sustaining grudges left. Perhaps his anti-Semitism was by then respectable, in the English manner, and not a reflection of his creative self-loathing.

In the closing pages of his books Anthony Julius tells how "the poet and man of letters Emanuel Litvinoff read to a London audience his poem 'To T. S. Eliot'. Eliot was present". After the reading, there was a protest from Stephen Spender on Eliot's behalf, but Eliot himself was heard to mutter generously, "It's a good poem, it's a very good poem". Here is Litvinoff's poem, written – like Julius's book – out of "resistance as well as respect":

I am not one accepted in your parish.
Bleistein is my relative and I share
the protozoic slime of Shylock, a page
in Stürmer, and, underneath the cities,
a billet somewhat lower than the rats.
Blood in the sewers. Pieces of our flesh
float with the ordure on the Vistula.

THE CLASSIC POEM

1. SELECTED BY FLEUR ADCOCK

GAVIN EWART DIED in October 1995, a few months short of his 80th birthday. (See John Whitworth's appreciation in *PR* Vol 85 No 4). I have chosen one of his 'So-called Sonnets' – so called by himself to distinguish them from traditional examples of the genre. It was not that he couldn't make sonnets rhyme and scan: there was no verse form he could not handle, and probably almost none he had never attempted in his enormously prolific later years. He wrote a verse saga in the form of 'The Wreck of the Deutschland'; he got his students on poetry courses to write serious limericks, and wrote some himself. He is a salutary example to those of us who mope around complaining that we haven't written very much recently because we didn't feel inspired or weren't in the mood. Gavin got up every morning, had breakfast, and then, unless he had to be somewhere else that day, sat down at his desk and wrote poems – about absolutely everything. Inevitably the quality varied; he wrote a good deal of cheerful rubbish, some of it forgettable or better forgotten. He also wrote much that was admirable, enjoyable, or startling, and some brilliant pieces which have long been classics of their kind. Among other things, he was a great entertainer.

However, this sonnet shows another side of the Ewart persona: his humanity. There is no show-off play with rhyme and metre, and no effort to dazzle or shock. The calm, almost flat tone and flexible speech rhythms are perfectly judged for the haunting subject-matter.

Fleur Adcock gained a degree of notoriety in the press with her poem 'A Political Kiss' (published in *PR*, Vol 85 No 3).

GAVIN EWART
SONNET: HOW LIFE TOO IS SENTIMENTAL

When our son was a few weeks old he had bronchial trouble
and picked up a cross-infection in the hospital
(salmonella typhimurium) through sluttish feeding –
but a hospital never admits it's responsible –
and was rushed away behind glass in an isolation ward,
at the point, it might be, of death. Our daughter,
eighteen months old, was just tall enough
to look into his empty cot and say: "Baby gone!"

A situation, an action and a speech
so tear-jerking that Dickens might have thought of them –
and indeed, in life, when we say "It couldn't happen!"
almost at once it happens. And the word "sentimental"
has come to mean exaggerated feeling.
It would have been hard to exaggerate *our* feelings then.

Reprinted by permission of Margot Ewart from *The Collected Ewart 1933–1980*.

2. SELECTED BY PETER REDGROVE

HAROLD BLOOM IN *The Poems of Our Climate* dislikes this "famous and over-rated set-piece" and plays down the fact that its subject is Stevens' great theme of the "crossing" or transformation from fancy to imagination. Helen Vendler, on the other hand, in her Hodges Lecture *Words Chosen Out of Desire* says that "The daily impersonal newness of the visible world was at first a disturbing thought to Stevens ... But now, at the end of his life, that aesthetic inexhaustibility of the world and the emotions is Stevens' only principle of faith". For me, 'Sea Surface' crept out over the radio in Guy Kingsley Poynter's voice in Cambridge in the 1950's while I was struggling with a philosophy course, baffled why the philosophers did not take into account exactly this prime datum of inexhaustible changeability in all their questionings of whether a table, say, was there or not. The poem intervened, miraculously unfolding on the air and evolving a qualitative difference out of the shallow logical-positivist despair of mere fantasy. The perplexed suavity mutated into living sea-blooms; the sham and malevolent flatness energised into crystalline pendentives; an uncertain green decided on a blue beyond the rainy hyacinth; the malice of dank stratagems foamed and thought; and the motley clown of the obese machine proceeded to freshest transformations. Who was responsible? Why, the poetic self, *mon frère du ciel*, and the depression in an enormous undulation fled. Conscious and unconscious mirror each other, the high and the low, as in Rimbaud: "Eternity / It is the sea / Mixed with the sun". Stevens' poem is still a model of poetic experience to me, as is is the majority of his work, living as I do by the eventful ocean of Falmouth.

Peter Redgrove's new book, *Assembling a Ghost*, is due out from Cape in November.

WALLACE STEVENS
SEA SURFACE FULL OF CLOUDS

I

In that November off Tehuantepec,
The slopping of the sea grew still one night
And in the morning summer hued the deck

And made one think of rosy chocolate
And gilt umbrellas. Paradisal green
Gave suavity to the perplexed machine

Of ocean, which like limpid water lay.
Who, then, in that ambrosial latitude
Out of the light evolved the moving blooms,

Who, then, evolved the sea-blooms from the clouds
Diffusing balm in that Pacific calm?
C'était mon enfant, mon bijou, mon âme.

The sea-clouds whitened far below the calm
And moved, as blooms move, in the swimming green
And in its watery radiance, while the hue

Of heaven in an antique reflection rolled
Round those flotillas. And sometimes the sea
Poured brilliant iris on the glistening blue.

II

In that November off Tehuantepec
The slopping of the sea grew still one night.
At breakfast jelly yellow streaked the deck

And made one think of chop-house chocolate
And sham umbrellas. And a sham-like green
Capped summer-seeming on the tense machine

Of ocean, which in sinister flatness lay.
Who, then, beheld the rising of the clouds
That strode submerged in that malevolent sheen,

Who saw the mortal massives of the blooms
Of water moving on the water-floor?
C'était mon frère du ciel, ma vie, mon or.

The gongs rang loudly as the windy booms
Hoo-hooed it in the darkened ocean-blooms.
The gongs grew still. And then blue heaven spread

Its crystalline pendentives on the sea
And the macabre of the water-glooms
In an enormous undulation fled.

III

In that November off Tehuantepec,
The slopping of the sea grew still one night
And a pale silver patterned on the deck

And made one think of porcelain chocolate
And pied umbrellas. An uncertain green,
Piano-polished, held the tranced machine

Of ocean, as a prelude holds and holds.
Who, seeing silver petals of white blooms
Unfolding in the water, feeling sure

Of the milk within the saltiest spurge, heard, then,
The sea unfolding in the sunken clouds?
Oh! C'était mon extase et mon amour.

So deeply sunken were they that the shrouds,
The shrouding shadows, made the petals black
Until the rolling heaven made them blue,

A blue beyond the rainy hyacinth,
And smiting the crevasses of the leaves
Deluged the ocean with a sapphire blue.

IV

In that November off Tehuantepec
The night-long slopping of the sea grew still.
A mallow morning dozed upon the deck

And made one think of musky chocolate
And frail umbrellas. A too-fluent green
Suggested malice in the dry machine

Of ocean, pondering dank stratagem.
Who then beheld the figures of the clouds
Like blooms secluded in the thick marine?

Like blooms? Like damasks that were shaken off
From the loosed girdles in the spangling must.
C'était ma foi, la nonchalance divine.

The nakedness would rise and suddenly turn
Salt masks of beard and mouths of bellowing,
Would – But more suddenly the heaven rolled

Its bluest sea-clouds in the thinking green,
And the nakedness became the broadest blooms,
Mile-mallows that a mallow sun cajoled.

V

In that November off Tehuantepec
Night stilled the slopping of the sea. The day
Came, bowing and voluble, upon the deck,

Good clown ... One thought of Chinese chocolate
And large umbrellas. And a motley green
Followed the drift of the obese machine

Of ocean, perfected in indolence.
What pistache one, ingenious and droll,
Beheld the sovereign clouds as jugglery

And the sea as turquoise-turbaned Sambo, neat
At tossing saucers – cloudy-conjuring sea?
C'était mon esprit bâtard, l'ignominie.

The sovereign clouds came clustering. The conch
Of loyal conjuration trumped. The wind
Of green blooms turning crisped the motley hue

To clearing opalescence. Then the sea
And heaven rolled as one and from the two
Came fresh transfigurings of freshest blue.

Reprinted by permission of Faber & Faber Ltd from Wallace Stevens,
Collected Poems.

A SECOND LOOK

Use Your Loaf

PHILIP GROSS ON A POET WHOSE WORK IS "A COMMANDO COURSE IN LANGUAGE"

N. H. REEVE & RICHARD KERRIDGE
Nearly Too Much:
The Poetry of J. H. Prynne

Liverpool University Press,
hbk £25.00 ISBN 0 85323 840 5
pbk £11.95 ISBN 0 85323 850 2

As what next if you can't, silent fire
dumped in a skip and sun boiling over
the sack race. Best before too late, with
loath to depart in the buff envelope torn across.

HERE IS THE problem of Prynne in a nutshell: the abrupt disruptions, fragments of the conversational ("what next?") cheek by jowl with the poetic "loath to depart", the Best Before date and the buff envelope next to the "silent fire", a haunting image in the urban "dumped in a skip" that still plausibly connects to "sun boiling over" . . . till the bathos of "the sack race" trips it up. Even that innocent "over" has its grammatical function thrown into doubt. Above all there is the refusal simply to make sense.

The problem is not just the British reading public's shyness of postmodern slips and shifts. John Ashbery sells well. But where Ashbery lulls us with that whimsical, ruminative speaking voice, the effect of Prynne is dry and spiky, almost aggressive in the way it jolts the reader out of any continuity. Sixty this year, he has been a presence since the 60s, on one fringe of English poetry with a stronghold of influence in Cambridge, and among critics who "foreground language". But almost all of his books are out of print. Only his first, *Force of Circumstance* (1962), which he excludes from his collected *Poems* (1982), had a major publisher; since then, his work has appeared from small presses, or self-published or in small-circulation magazines. The closest he has come to exposure was his central role in the Carcanet anthology *A Various Art*. Yet his presence is real, a watchword for difficulty and intransigence,

a challenge to received ideas of poetry. In short, a problem, something to be reckoned with.

If you think that context will supply the answers to the lines above, from *The Oval Window* (1983), think again. The same teasing reappearances, snatched away at once, occur throughout the 27-page poem. Maybe "think again" is the point, on a line-by-line, phrase-by-phrase basis. This is a very special claim to make for poetry. In any other kind of human interaction, such wilful refusal to communicate would make the other party walk away. Why should we stay to wrestle with it on the page? This book is as close as most of us will get to an answer – not an easy one. Prynne is an academic, fiercely intellectual, and if we are not prepared to meet him on that ground we will not meet at all. This is not *The Rough Guide to J. H. Prynne*. Reeve and Kerridge do write with remarkable clarity, given their subject and given the theory they bring to bear on him. Anyone wanting to get to grips with Bakhtin, Habermas, Kristeva, the new critical canon, should read the chapter where each of these approaches is explained in action and with reference to Prynne.

This book offers no easy way through the back door of biography. Even when motifs – that of physical decay and wounds, for example – cry out for some personal connection, it is not to be had . . . in deference maybe to Prynne's constant struggle to decentre his poems from the individual. What we do meet is Prynne on the page, and the sight of the authors themselves wrangling with the text. This is of course what critical theory demands; it is also a labour of love. The authors can express frustration at the commando-course of language a Prynne poem is, but it must be respect for the man and his work that keeps them engaged, ten pages at a time devoted to opening up a single poem. You see their love, too, of the intellectual exercise this sort of poetry becomes. I have never got closer to understanding what Barthes might have meant by *le plaisir du texte* than watching the authors picking their way through the seemingly endlessly deferred gratification of the poem 'Royal Fern'. At the end I reread it myself and found myself joining in: but you must not expect definitive interpretations; it is an introduction to a world where there are none, a world of not arriving, but travelling hopefully. There are useful directions, though. One chapter shows how regularly Prynne splices the human scale, the traditional homeland of poetry, up against the huge (geological processes, or macro-economics) and the minute. Subjective language is brought up hard against the scientific (though to identify science with pure objectivity seems touchingly old-fashioned these days, especially when Marxist economics figures as a *science*). What the effect is, is another matter. Prynne, after all, selects his samples of metallurgy or computer jargon or advertising slogans and cuts and pastes at will. The effect, for me at least, is often irony or pathos. Don't we stick by the human even when, or especially when, it is threatened by dizzying contrasts of scale?

As for contrasts of language –

From the skip there is honey and bent metal,
romantic on trade plates: PUT SKIP EDIT,
PUT SKIP DATA, the control flow structure
demands a check that subscripts do not exceed
array dimensions . . .

– many of Prynne's language-samples are "linguistic gestures" (as Kerridge and Reeve themselves say). Deconstruction calls on us to see language "exposed as a system, not inhabited as utterance". The effect can be caricature, to label a way of speaking rather than explore what could actually be said in it.

For all the stress on objectivity, there is a moralistic core to this account of Prynne. This goes deeper than political judgements (both shaving soap and lawnmowers get designated "bourgeois"). There is a Puritan rigour in Prynne's refusal to allow any moment of feeling or sense-contact to exist for long enough for any of us to inhabit it, at least not for more than an instant. The authors recommend a steadfast refusal of the "consolation" offered by a finished poem, centring on human experience and offering it a shape. Prynne's recurrent image of the wound becomes not only physical but an open wound in our consciousness, the impossibility of holding the fragments of the world together. And the task of the thinker is to keep the wound open, not to help or heal it.

The paradox is that Prynne does an extraordi-

nary amount of thinking about feeling. His repeated use of single abstract words like "love" or "hope" or "fear" would be blue-pencilled instantly in your local creative writing class. (Which of the 57 varieties of "love" is he talking about?) Prynne's refusal to use imagery, concrete detail and anecdote to make the abstract real is a defiance. It is partly an attack on, partly sympathy for, the word. Against the chaos round it, what can a poor bare word like "Love" do?

And yet reading Prynne does leave a sense of hurts and yearnings, somewhere under the difficult argumentative surface. His refusal of consolation is an emotional strategy we recognise. Only someone who feels the need spends so much time in fighting it. The closing lines of *The Oval Window* read

Standing by the window I heard it,
while waiting for the turn. In hot light
and chill air it was the crossing flow
of even life, hurt in the mouth but
exhausted with passion and joy. Free
to leave at either side, at the fold line
found in threats like herbage, the watch
is fearful and promised before. The years
jostle and burn up as a trust plasma.
Beyond help it is joy at death itself:
a toy hard to bear, laughing all night.

This moves me and leaves me undecided. Is Prynne's tense wrestling with language the acceptance of an almost superhuman challenge, or a defence against the human business of dealing with what "love" or "hurt" might actually mean for us? In Prynne's world, with its Modernist ambition to shore fragments against the ruin of a unified world view, and its Postmodern disbelief in making anything cohere, both things might be true.

Meanwhile there is the wrangling. There are passages so dense with obliquities that far from the excitement of multiple meanings I just have the bleak feeling of ennui – *so what* – because any meaning might be equally possible. The constant puns and mangled clichés can recall the grim word-play of Geoffrey Hill's *Funeral Music* ("They bespoke doomsday and they meant it by / God") but *sans* the solemn music. Instead there is an effect like trawling the radio dial at random: a few bars of Classic FM, a snatch of lecture on Radio 3, a bit of babble from Talk Radio UK.

The authors of this book deserve credit for reminding us that there is humour in Prynne (titles like 'On the Matter of Thermal Packing', 'Rich in Vitamin C' or 'Use Your Loaf', which begins "Then part of it fell down. It was like rain, down was its fall . . .", a Wallace Stevens, even E. E. Cummings, moment which has got to be a tease). The title of this book nicely exposes lines from *Down where changed*: "Nearly too much / is, well, nowhere near enough". The first phrase may well be a new reader's reaction to a page of Prynne. The rest may be their reaction to the dedicated exposition of this book. But still, it is a start, done with such commitment, honesty and yes, love, that you might want to read on. Prynne's work should be more easily available, in case you do.

Philip Gross's latest collection is *I. D.* (Faber, 1995).

Bibliography

This list does not pretend to be exhaustive. Of these titles, only *The Oval Window* is currently listed in British Books in Print.

Force of Circumstance, Routledge, London, 1962
Kitchen Poems, Cape Goliard, London, 1968
Day Light Songs, R Books, Pampisford, 1968
Aristeas, Ferry Press, London, 1968
The White Stones, Grosseteste Press, Lincoln, 1969
Fire Lizard, Blacksuede Boot Press, Barnet, 1970
Brass, Ferry Press, London, 1971
Into the Day, Cambridge, privately printed, 1972
A Night Square, Albion Village Press, London, 1973
Wound Response, Street Editions, Cambridge, 1974

High Pink on Chrome, Cambridge, privately printed, 1975
News of Warring Clans, Trigram Press, London, 1977
Down where changed, Ferry Press, London, 1979
Poems, Agneau 2 (subsequently Allardyce. Barnett), Edinburgh & London, 1982
The Oval Window, Cambridge, privately printed, 1983
Bands Around The Throat, Cambridge, privately printed, 1987
Word Order, Prest Roots Press, Kenilworth, 1989
Not-You, Equipage, Cambridge, 1993
Her Weasels Wild Returning, Equipage, Cambridge, 1994

Web page

Nate Dorward, a Ph.D. student at Dalhousie University, has set up a J. H. Prynne homepage on http://ac.dal. ca/~ndorward/homepage.html

MICHAEL HENRY
SEARCHLIGHT TATTOO

When women unwrap the blue paper
from white tablecloths I think
of the surprising whiteness of salt
cupped in blue glass in a silver cellar.

My hands could make mountains of such whiteness
like a boy on his first day at the seaside
and I will bury my hands in the salt
and pack a white mask of No on my face

and scarify the threads of my veins
until the blood runs out blue.
And I will dip my pen in this well of blue ink
and write on the broadside of pages.

And I will twirl the blue paper into touchpaper
and light it in the dark blue light of the street
where passing faces are powdered with gunpowder
and needles drop off the trees like wishbones.

NEW POETS '96

EACH ISSUE THIS YEAR WILL FEATURE TWO OR THREE POETS
WHO HAVE YET TO PUBLISH A FULL COLLECTION

PAUL FARLEY

'WE MOVED AROUND a lot when I was very young, in Liverpool, before settling on an estate. My family were numerous, all ex-Canadian Pacific, ex-Cunard it seemed. I remember being happy, self-absorbed. School, especially later on, was a trial. After, someone suggested I should send some drawings and paintings to an art college. I got into Chelsea in 1985, which was fun, eye-opening. There was a theoretical curriculum, and though the stuff on the Frankfurt School probably fell on stony ground, I did get introduced to the work of Lowell, Berryman, Bishop and others (thanks, Stuart). After college I worked as a courier, cinema usher, scene painter and spider wrangler, before ending up in a library. The writing seems to have been there for a long time – fits and starts of bad prose, fanzine articles, then, over a couple of years ago, verse. I helped form a splinter group (still nameless) with people I met at Michael Donaghy's City University workshop. Since then there have been magazine appearances, readings, and a prize in the 1994 Bridport. I won first prize in the 1995 Arvon Competition.

SISTER

It's gone quiet – there is no more cursing
at the TV as his horse hits the fence.
The weather doesn't "turn gangster", simply worsens,
a black cloud moving in front of the sun.

We go to bed when we please – don't run for fags,
for bets, don't eat in silence. Set the canary free –
we don't need it risking his outhouse stink,
buoyant filter tip, offensive whistling . . .

And please, don't reject me when I come clean
and admit I've stolen his wink,
his facial tic. Don't be too quick to judge
my voice as it drops to his octave,

employs the odd kibosh, cahoots, buckshee.
Catch my myoclonic jerk
from a seconds-old dream about lifts or kerbs.
Something of him informs something of me.

WHY WAITRESSES CRY

All afternoon the chicane ribboned offside
Lit by our headlights. And I pulled over
After nearly taking us up the verge at eighty.
Coffee. More coffee. Endless cigarettes
Stretching back a week that seems as long
Or short as my watery mind's eye wants.
I almost killed us all dreaming of you,
Up the M4 with your three hour lead.

My passengers said I should get my head down.
I did. And I was a short order waitress
Sidling from kitchen to table with notepad
In hand, trying to write in between the demands
Of an egg-cracking cook and his customers
In that shorthand a doctor, dead on his feet,
Might employ; or a love note, slid on a beermat
Across the slops and ash of an evening.

And I carried the laminate, ersatz hidebound
Menu to your table, and asked what you wanted,
Or whatlyubehavin? And you recognised me,
Even dragged-up in gingham and paper hat,
Saw me coming. But nobody broached it
And so we went through the ritual of ordering;
Your sunny-side-up to my scribbling and nodding.
Clearing, I found a butt stubbed into yolk.

The car starts from cold. We press on in silence.
England at its most wipered, American state
Between services, runs off the windscreen.
Further ahead now, your junction, your turn-off,
And I'll keep my foot down until we reach London.
But not before several dangerous re-screenings
Are attempted, then aborted from the backseat:
My name's Paul. I'll be your waitress this evening . . .

STRAY

Whatever brought me to the gutter
Had something to do with this:
A tree-lined journey to the shop for booze,
Paracetamol and papers
Where I came across his name
On a photocopied flyer
Tacked to the bark of every other trunk.
I soon got to know his sooty coat,
Reflective collar. So tenderly written
I half-expected a *Last seen wearing* . . .

Someone had added *Try the Peking Garden*
In shaky freehand. There was a reward
So I started to keep an eye out.
When you asked me what I was thinking
Staring into a darkening tangle
Those evenings we sat outside drinking
It was usually to do with him –
Slowly turning to mulch in deep thicket;
Eaten alive by pit bulls;
A carbon copy given to a child

Who thought him lost to the night.
We'd take in the chairs. I'd sit in the window
Listening to far-off sirens
And the sound of my breathing. He was stretching,
Getting used to the name they'd given him.
It grew, until one night in September
We ran low on smokes. You sent me to the garage.
I walked down that road with the trees
Heavy and still. Hardly a whisper. Turned
Past the all-nighter and kept on walking.

THE ORAL ROUTE

What am I trying to do here? I tell him talking
Cures will do me no good, I've tried them.
Now he squeaks apart his leather clasp case
And goes through the motions – a cold stethoscope,
Pulse compared to his wristwatch, patella hammer . . .
I'm trying to steer him to the right diagnosis:

An uncontrollable urge to sleep, doc. Any time of day
Or night. I'm watching autumn through the blinds
Then I'm in its thrall. I always go past my stop.
I worry about hibernation. One day I'll wake up
In spring. I've tried cold baths, proper coffee,
The house is full of alarm clocks. Help me beat this.

The doctor stares through his surgery window –
Somewhere in the Punjab, to the north late snow lies
On the peaks and the warm afternoon drones endless to
The scent of smoke and asafoetida. I am his favourite
"Fat envelope", in every week. In his dream
I'm sketching my dreary prognosis by rote.

A bicycle dusts up the path. He signs for the envelope.
He holds it to the light, then tears it apart.
Results . . . I have stopped talking, doc. Your turn now.
He swivels back, to me, to the cries of children
Brought in from the tower blocks. With a practised hand
He writes out a script for another placebo.

Andrew Herbert

IAN PARKS

IAN PARKS WAS BORN in Mexborough, South Yorkshire in 1959. A pamphlet collection, which received a Yorkshire Arts Award, was published by Littlewood in 1985. From 1986-88 he was Writer-in-Residence at North Riding College, Scarborough, and went on to teach creative writing for the WEA at the Universities of Sheffield and Hull. Recent poems have appeared in *Bête Noire, Oxford Poetry, Poetry Wales, The Rialto, Oxford Magazine, English, New Voices in British Poetry* (California University Press), and have been broadcast on BBC Radio 3. He received a Hawthornden Fellowship in 1991 and a Travelling Fellowship to the United States in 1993. He came third in the 1994 City of Cardiff International Poetry Competition and won the Cascando travel prize to Prague in 1995. He lives in Oxford and is currently working on a first novel.

ATLANTIC HOUSE

Here, on the western seaboard,
things affirm their close affinity
with light. A haunted cottage
at the water's edge, where night
after night you slept with me,

our room a landlocked cabin –
closed, confined – and all
our acts of love took place
within earshot of the sea.
So much was unexplained:

tread the floorboards, you could hear
the creak of timbers overhead,
rigging cast a shadow on the wall,
a strange hook twisted down
above the bed. We tilted

on the sand-bank easily.
The sun sank early, making room
for those who'd gone before
like us to watch its furious light
dispersing iridescence in the bay.

We learned a new vocabulary
of compass, log-book, chart;
a beach of stones and shingle
stretched away. I loved you,
so I let the tide begin

its slow erosion into nothingness.
Under the beams, our ghosts
are kissing still. I see
you on the shore in your white dress,
turning as you did after the dance

and take with me the salt-taste
of your eyes; a smooth grey pebble
for a paperweight. When all else fails
I haul my sheets onto the ledge
and let the wind fill out my sails.

THE GIRL FROM WEST VIRGINIA

I met her on a Greyhound
heading south, still smarting
from the decades of defeat.
We shared a can of Miller
and she smiled. Her snake-belt buckle
showed in bold relief
the high-tide of the Civil War –
a thin grey line at Gettysburg;
the southern army going down
in fields of harvest wheat –
and under it, in Rebel red and blue,
The South Will Rise Again.
Snow veered across the windscreen.
Drugstores and graveyards
broke the white; Old Glory frozen
on a pole. Her red-check shirt,
her careless smile, she reminded me of you.
New England is a Greyhound
heading south, and the girl
from West Virginia coming through.

OVERNIGHT

For weeks they slept together in the heart
of the frozen city. Down in the street
the troops limped past on ice. Statues
were shattered in the public squares;

voices fell silent in the afternoons.
For the first time now they slept apart:
from his high attic room with the fractured pane
he squinted at the far grey quarter

where she lay awake, turning her dark
familiar head under pale domes and spires.
At the station, when he stooped to kiss
goodbye, she found the button of his uniform

and slipped a hand inside his shirt.
Next morning they woke up to find
the wires were down, the barriers manned,
and all love's interchange cut short.

RUTH SHARMAN

I WAS BORN IN MADRAS, where my father was a tanner. He collected butterflies and I learnt to share his love of the natural world. At six I was taken from the heat and the flame trees to a place where what mattered was tying your shoelaces and telling the time – and I was laughed at because I could do neither. I spent the next twenty years trying to "catch up", never succeeding, despite a double first in Modern Languages from Cambridge. I stayed on to do a Ph.D., but these were bleak years, during which I wore my academic achievements as a kind of mask and was frequently ill. My mother died suddenly during this time and it was the pain of losing her that prompted my first tentative poems. Marriage and psychoanalysis have helped me to write in the last three years, and through writing I have come to feel more solid, as if the blank spaces inside had been coloured in. After what seemed like early flukes – second prize in the Arvon (1989); runner-up in the National (1990) – I have had poems published in the *Sunday Times, Observer, Independent, London Magazine, Poetry Review*, and *The Faber Book of Murder*, and a selection is due to appear in the Staple First Editions series next summer. When I am not writing poetry, I work as a freelance translator.

ILLUSTRATIONS OF THE BRITISH FLORA

My father bought me this sober little book
when I was still too young to comprehend
the reproductive processes in flowers,
its references to ovules, perianths and angiosperms.

The plates showed in black and white a hundred
varieties of grass and puzzled us with Compositae
and Umbellifers that were hard to tell apart,
encouraging a "Spot the Difference" of our own.

After each walk I'd colour in another vetch or daisy,
blurring the edges like an old lady's lipstick,
adding "Nobottle Woods" or "marsh" or "disused railway"
in writing that joined up with the years.

The book was my bible, symbol of a private dialogue
with my dad (who always did talk best through things)
and as I look at the crinkled creamy pages,
at all the blank spaces among the brightness

I want to see those missing flowers filled in
and write the names for places we never knew
until each page is thick with ink and pastel
and all that was left unsaid is said in silence now.

MUMMY

Dearest, we'll start by removing
the bits you won't need any more

– just a delicate cut,
before bathing you inside and out –

then we'll sweeten your flesh
with cinnamon, cedar and myrrh.

So you shine like a god, we'll wrap leaves
of electrum round fingers and toes,

and those muscular shoulders and legs
we'll keep toned

by secreting soft shavings
just under the skin.

We'll preserve you in crystals of natron
and bathe you again.

Then we'll bind. Do it finger
by finger,

and strap down those hands that have strayed,
in a cross at your heart.

With your torso and limbs we'll arrange
a neat parcel in lattice designs

while reserving the narrowest bands
for your head,

which we'll wrap from the left,
then the right, the same number of times,

gently sealing those lips that have lied
with the linen's soft kiss.

Once you're upright, I'll breathe
through your mouth

and I'll open your eyes
to a world in which nothing has changed.

All around will be things that you know.
You'll have garlands and honey with milk

while that niche by the door
will be perfectly placed

for watching me come
and then go.

TOUCH

That was the garden where I'd ride horses
whose names I'd heard on TV
and written in my private book,
and where I planted London Pride and trimmed
a two-foot square of lawn with bathroom scissors.

From the plum tree I could see the sky
and look across the fields that rolled up
to our garden fence and down to where
a curve of trees followed the contours
of the hills and hid a stream

I'd spend hours damming and undamming,
where only water sounds would break
the stillness or a sudden flash
of wings, and in spring a mass of violets
flowered in the shadows, scented, white.

There were three of us building dams
the day the big boys came and told us
to take off our clothes and *Touch. Go on, touch,*
so we shackled our knees with trouser legs
and touched each other in places
                    we'd not touched before.

They laughed, kicked a stone or two and left . . .
We watched as water seeped at first,
then prised apart all that our hands had done
and the whole muddy torrent came bursting through
with its cargo of leaves and scum.

IN APPRECIATION OF

George Mackay Brown 1921–1996

by Iain Crichton Smith

FIRST NORMAN MacCAIG and now George Mackay Brown. The ranks of senior Scottish poets are beginning to thin alarmingly.

George Mackay Brown died on the 13th April in Kirkwall hospital. He had never been strong physically (in his youth he had T.B.) and much of his work was done while not in good health. Latterly he never left the Orkneys though in earlier days he could be found in the pubs in Edinburgh along with other poets of the time such as MacCaig himself. He spent a very happy time in Newbattle Abbey during the period when the other famous Orcadian poet, Edwin Muir, was in charge there. They were however in my opinion quite different as poets, Muir reverting to Troy for much of his inspiration, Mackay Brown to Orkney's Viking past.

Two years ago, he was shortlisted for the Booker Prize but didn't go to London for the final prize-giving ceremony; he said he would feel out of place among the literati there. He was never to be dazzled by cosmopolitan glitter and though he received many awards and honours he remained entirely unassuming. He thought of himself as a craftsman: his life and art seemed a seamless garment. Unlike many writers his ego was very tiny (if it existed at all) and he was always generous to the young. In summertime his house was invaded by fans from all over the world and he had to leave, I believe, his council flat where, though he was hostile to much technology (believing for instance that TV had destroyed an oral culture), he was in fact surrounded by the usual gadgetry.

He was like the bard of earlier times in the role he played in the Orkneys. He memorialised its Viking history, its bloodthirsty past and to a lesser extent its calmer present. He saw the Orcadian in his double role as ploughman and fisherman. Behind the novelist and short story writer was ultimately the poet. He composed a mythology out of tinkers, seamen, lairds and ministers. It was on the whole a radiant world that he wrote of, a world of the seasons, a heraldic world, shot through with images of sun and water and corn and his Catholic faith, for he was a Catholic convert. His religion made him an optimistic writer, though he could write of nuclear threat and potential destruction. But in general his world was one which had true significance. His style in poetry was unique. He began with echoes of Gerald Manley Hopkins (whom he had studied) but progressed to his own true voice. This made him write a lapidary poetry built up as if it were one stone line on another, with an excised feel about it. Sometimes he would write calendar poems, sometimes poems which commemorated people. Key words were "ale", "corn", "bread" etc. Numbers too were often used, such as "seven fish" or "three horsemen". The world in front of him was fresh and real but it was also penetrated by a very deeply felt and visualised past. George scanned over and over the book of nature that lay before him; it was extraordinary how fruitful he found an area which to others might seem limited. He saw the world as holy because of his Catholic faith and perhaps as pagan too because of the intense lives that his brawling ancestors led.

He did not write much about modern Orkney except in the weekly column that he wrote for *The Orcadian* and even there he wrote much of the seasons and historical names of places. He took his walk every day in Stromness and of course was a familiar figure. Looking at Orkney now one can see a huge gap opening in it, for he mythologised the island and made of it an imaginative world. He was entirely at home there. He even used to make his own beer. Like MacCaig his death was widely commemorated by the media: he had reached out beyond the normal readership of poetry and prose. His prose was lucid and poetic, he was a very fine short story writer. The style of his poetry was original and instantly recognisable. His latest book

Following a Lark begins with one of his great themes, the conflict between book learning and knowledge of nature. It is about a boy being gathered into school against his will. Says the boy:

> Jimmo Spence, he told me
>> where the lark's nest is,
>> beside a stone in his father's oatfield,
>> the high granite corner.

George Mackay Brown was undoubtedly one of Scotland's greatest writers of the twentieth century, radiant, life-affirming and accessible. Perhaps he was greatest of all as a short story writer but, as I have said, beneath and behind all his work lie the insights and illuminations of poetry.

Iain Crichton Smith's *Collected Poems* is reviewed on page 84. George Mackay Brown's last book, *Following a Lark* (John Murray, £8.99) was published in April.

GEORGE MACKAY BROWN
ROBERT RENDALL
ORKNEY POET

You have been here, before your latest birth,
    (Cheeks, at the pan-pipes, apple-red and round!)
Followed your wooden plough through Attic earth,
    And pulled your lobsters from a wine-dark sound.

– Now for a flicker of time you walk once more
    In other islands, under geese-gray skies,
And note, on Birsay hill and Birsay shore,
    The year's glad cycle out of ancient eyes.

O happy grove of poetry! where the soul
    Is never sundered from the laughing blood,
But sweetly bound, harmonious and whole
    In covenant with animal and god.

But I came here unheralded, and meet
Masquers and shadows mingling in the street.

Reprinted by permission of John Murray Ltd from George Mackay Brown, *Following a Lark*.

PAUL MULDOON
LONGBONES

When she came to me that night in Damascus Street
she was quite beside herself. Her father was about to die
and his mirror was covered with a sheet

so his spirit might not beat
against it but fly as spirits fly.
When she came to me that night in Damascus Street

Longbones had driven through freezing rain or sleet
all the way from Lurgan. The Lurgan sky
was a mirror covered with a sheet

or a banner trailed by an army in defeat.
Though Longbones was already high
when she came to me that night in Damascus Street

she immediately shook out a neat
little blue or red cartouche until, by and by,
she had covered a mirror with a sheet

of that most valiant dust. Then she would entreat
me not to leave her, as if I
had come to her that night in Damascus Street,

as if I had asked if I might turn up the heat
and tested if the spare bed was dry
by slipping the mirror between the sheets.

Only when she turned to greet
me, wistful and wry,
that night of nights in Damascus Street,

did I remark on the discreet
blue or red teardrop tattooed under her left eye.
She covered the mirror with a sheet

and whispered, "come, my sweet",
in a tone as sly as it was shy,
"come to me now". That night in Damascus Street

was the last time Longbones and I would meet.
Only later did it strike me why
she would cover the mirror with a sheet.

Only when I looked back on her snow-white feet
and her snow-white thigh
did it come to me, next morning in Damascus Street,
that she herself was the mirror covered with a sheet.

HELEN DUNMORE

HE LIVED NEXT DOOR ALL HIS LIFE

One year he painted his front door yellow.
It was the splash of a carrier bag
in the dun terrace,
but for the rest he was inconspicuous.

He went out one way and came back the other,
often carrying laundry and once compost
for the tree he thought might do in the back yard.
Some time later there was its skeleton
taking up most of the bin.

He passed the remark "It's a pity"
when it rained on a Saturday,
and of a neighbour's child he said "terror".
He picked his words like scones from a plate,

dropping no crumbs. When his front door shut
he was more gone than last Christmas.
But for the girls stored in his basement
to learn what it meant
to have no pity, to be terror,
he was there.

MICHAEL DONAGHY
THE PALM

la connaissance aux cent passages – René Char

That motorcycle downstairs never starts
but, like a statue with a stomach flu,
disturbs him with its monumental farts.
His phone won't stop. His arts review is due
and must be in the post by half past three
to make this issue of *Je Suis Partout*.
And here's another *merde* to fuel his rage:
he has to wrestle with a rusty key.
Though they assured him this machine was new,
he's got to press the "j" against the page
whenever he types *jazz* or *Juiverie*
and he uses these words frequently.
It jams again, the phone rings. Bang on cue,
The motorcycle starts. The curtains part
on the Palm Casino, 1942.

> Although he thinks she's buying out the town
> the critic's wife sits on an unmade bed
> in room 6, naked, as her palm is read
> by a guitarist in a dressing gown.
> He reels off lines in the forgotten script
> that maps her palm: *Here is your first affair...*
> He looks at her but she can't help but stare
> down at the hand in which her hand is gripped.

Re-thinking his title, "For the Masses"
typewriter underarm, the critic passes
in the hallway a trolley of caramelised pears
and a fat man with a string bass case who stares
suspiciously back behind dark glasses.
Could this be M. Vola, room 9, who plays
that nigger music for Vichy gourmets,
hunting the Gypsy guitarist in his band?
The critic squints to memorise his face
as the lift cage rattles open for Vola and his bass.
Voila! He'll call it "Rhetoric and Race".

But back to those pears. Glazed, tanned,
they fall in behind a whole roast pig
delivered to the Gypsy's room before the gig.
He watches the waiter watch his crippled hand
as, with the other, he tries to sign his name.
He's new at this. It never looks the same.

The typewriter? Dismantled. All the keys
arranged across a workbench side by side.
And the critic hissing *Can I have your name please?*
and *What do you mean you're not qualified?*
and *Shall we call the police judiciaire?*
Tomorrow he will not be everywhere.

Tonight the Gypsy counts in the Quintet.
They'll play until the curfew lifts at dawn.
They have to call this foxtrot "*La Soubrette*"
but it's "*I've Got My Love To Keep Me Warm*".

PETER SNOWDON
DESIGN FOR LOVING

That summer Proust lay sleeping on his shelf.
On the mantlepiece an ormolu clock
Chimed with its reflection. Its chinless face
Overlooked oceans of red piling up

At the feet of two small china dogs
Who cocked their smooth heads and tried to look away,
Embarrassed. Cut stems of roses splayed,
Entwined themselves, drowning deliciously in the thick

Turbulent pelt. The window's sash-jaw sagged,
A sheepbone emptied of its light,
Denting the small white pillows strewn across

Your great-aunt's bed. I watched as creases crashed
Above me, and your laughter shone, spinning out
Into the afternoon, still unwritten and unread.

CHRISTINE DESPARDES
THE PARACHUTE

The changing of the guard is taking place,
so set your clocks an hour ahead to-day.

From cyberspace beyond the Baltic, like
the ripples on the sea, more calls arrive;
it's five, though, and I'd like to leave.

That very small hotel by the canal,
the northern lights, and then a madrigal
of Palestrina's. Then, that French café,
a violin, a steak with Beaujolais.

A toast to *Star Trek* on TV! A grain
of sand, our earth, too tiny to explain,
remote within this twirling galaxy,
alone at risk, and fleeting. And then he
walks in. The one who just walked in before.
I'm mesmerized. My wineglass hits the floor.
That stranger. Max. The one whom I adore.

Just every city is a jungle, Rome
in her declining days. Barbarians
are at the very gate. But here, at home,
man in the fulness of his being stands.

He's injured, though, his hand is dripping blood.
First aid comes easily to me. The bar-
tender pours Max an ice-cold Bud
for free. Two crackheads from the boulevard

are lying flat upon their backs outside.
The mad decline since World War I, of pride,
of manners, of respect for learning, all
have petered out and ceased to be. Recall

Atlantis, how she sank into the deep.
Legend alone remains about the gods
who walked among us then. What are the odds
that there once was a world we'll never see?

Not long ago, five years, perhaps, before
you came to be? The spacemen that we meet
in cave paintings, the Pyramids, what's more –
Why should a city sink beneath the sea ...?

PATRICIA TYRRELL
THE BODY'S TRACE ELEMENTS

"Here's gold", as fraying maps proclaim.
I've mined in you without noticing these elements
quiet as icons in the mystery of your flesh.

What have we to do with grey-sheened zinc,
magnesium flare, copper skillet,
the salt lash of the sea,
the wince of chlorinated public baths,
a rusting iron rod,
volcano's yellow-sulphur calyx,
the painter's cobalt lure,
steel-tough molybdenum,
hint of manganese –
and the gold in us, the gold?

I could sell you tomorrow
or you me, in any Commodities market
for roughly two-pounds-fifty sterling
based on the price of minerals that day.

Morning arrives like scales to calculate us.
You're first up. Where you've lain,
warmth generated by our double chemistries
teases, insinuates, like an explaining,
not fool's-gold heat but the rare metal's.
I turn my lips to the shaped hollow
and, two rooms off, your singing
structures our complex new experiment.

TONY CURTIS
THE EIGHTH DREAM

First he fingers wet sand into the names –
his hand traces the letters, then the numbers
of the squadron, then the boy's home state.
Sand spills into other names and numbers
above and below. He wipes the line
smooth with a sponge; then with an artist's brush
flicks away the final lodged grains.

This is the way to raise the dead
for the photograph the relatives receive.
It is fifty years and those who remembered
have phoned or faxed for flowers to be laid:
a wreath under one of the columns of the dead
where that long-lost brother holds his place
in the alphabet of the missing.

It is the end of the first week of December –
a brushing of snow highlights the grass
and softens the Portland stone walls of remembrance.
The rectangular ponds have coffin-lids of ice.
The stars and stripes is moulded to its towering pole,
the point from which the headstones radiate
their Roman Crosses and Stars of David.

These are the boys whose masks were torn apart,
Whose blood froze in the high air over Berlin,
Dresden and Cologne. Whose minced bodies were hosed out
over the warm fuselage in a Cambridgeshire field.
The ones who died slowly by an open window, listening
to strange birdsong. Those who ploughed into the runway fog.
Sailors who gagged on diesel and salt in the dark
Atlantic, and were numbed out of life.
They were the numbers on the walls
behind the Enigma boffins, Christ's and King's men
unscrambling the alphabet in Bletchley's Nissen huts.

Eighth Air Force fliers had a target of missions
that shifted – twenty, thirty, thirty-five –
always away from them as targets and statistics
were chalked across the wall of the hut.
Write it down, write it down.
They used their Zippos to burn into the pub's ceiling
memorials of crashed numbers and friends.

In the torn or frozen moment
they dreamed of a rusty red barn in Leverett,
the endless runway of roads across Oklahoma,
a foghorn in pain off Provincetown.
Their fiftieth winter in Heaven sees this present
dream of snow, the opaque, unreflecting ice,
and, in all the bare trees, one bright sweetgum,
that liquidambar of fall in the low, rinsed sun.

IAIN BAMFORTH
GOING OUT

(after Rilke)

Time and again we go out, hope in our heads,
though we know each bield and outhouse
in the landscape of love, the granite terraces

with their rhones and gables, the mercat cross
looking slackly down on what it means to be
home, fresh-puffed-up clouds amassing

time and again, though we know the poky
vandalised kirk and its attitudinising messenger,
pitfalls and flacks and sporting shibboleths

appointed to guy us, still we go out
hand in hand, imminent in a crowd of kids
and flapping parents, to the improbably giant

fossilized trees where we rest for the duration,
coats off in the bracken, ogling the sky.

CAROLE SATYAMURTI
LES AUTRES OR MR BLEANEY'S OTHER ROOM

Hell is a hotel bedroom, and other people,
implicit in the trapped, pine-freshened air,
fill you with their discomforts – room not quite
warm enough, bed intolerant. It's clear

you're one of a sad company who've seen
themselves wrapped up by chintz and candlewick,
who've spat in this basin, interrogated this
same toilet bowl for signs; or, maybe, sick

of their own company, turned on TV
and tried to feel drama or panel game
might give a handle on some richer life,
but found the room immured them just the same.

And you, like them, lie squeamish on the sheet
that veils the map of other people's lust,
fever, clumsiness, incontinence;
toss, sleepless and resentful, under musty

blankets' meagre weight, and realise
how you have buttressed your identity
with fragile props, convinced yourself of your
uniqueness. Foolish. You'll see – when you die

you'll land up in the final hotel bedroom,
where your mucus, dandruff, pubic hairs and sweat
will (but for the finer print of DNA)
turn out to be like anyone's you've met.

And though to swallow your disgust and breathe
deeply the air you share with everyone,
as if you loved them, might transform a hell
into a kind of heaven – can it be done?

JOHN DIXON
"ANOTHER EMPTY ROOM"
(SONG OF THE FORM MISTRESS AT 40 ODD)

There's nothing left for me to do
but teach the things I never learned.
Abortion: if it brushes *you*
ensure your after-shave's returned.
I didn't; which is why I'm not
the Mrs. that you might expect;
just plain Miss Squeeze who can't exhort
a uterus to that effect.

Although there have been other men
who put their savings into me
(before they took them out again
to realise a family).
Their sons refund me – more or less –
by overdrawing on their dreams
whenever they look down my dress
or re-inspect their natural creams.

Yet this is all I've left to show
for shuffling my life away.
As if I'd somewhere else to go,
or more important things to say.
It haunts me with another ten,
or twenty uninvited years
when now will be another then
and nowhere left to flaunt my tears.

The winter trees will be the same
as those that tussled with the air
that spare September when I came
and took their room into my care,
except that I'll have almost gone
from everywhere that means so much,
and yet so little once its done
I might not have occurred as such.

Although there was a moment when
I almost happened out of love
and half became myself again
like someone I'd been emptied of.
That time of me will always live
itself out to a life that I
have nothing left of to forgive
except the moment that I die.

THE REVIEW PAGES

Tribal Trojan Horse

by Fiachra Gibbons

SEAMUS HEANEY

The Spirit Level

Faber, £7.99,

ISBN 0571 17822 7

SEAMUS HEANEY'S NEW COLLECTION ticked away in my bag for a fortnight before I opened it. The problem with heroes is they let you down just when you least expect it. And the problem for Irish heroes, is that we keep shooting them for it. A knock on the door, a blindfold ride in the back of a car between men in balaclavas. A few encouraging blows around the head with the butt of a Biretta or the Collected Yeats, a lecture from Edna Longley, and then the chance to recant on tape for the sake of the relatives.

One of the dangers of canonisation is the martyrdom you're expected to endure for it. But Heaney had the glick to take the chair lift to Calvary and duck every cross thrust upon him. His halo has been hovering for long enough now that he can afford to wear it at a tilt. And you get the feeling that is what he intends to do.

His work has always been a struggle with reticence, not just political, but personal. A battle for self-expression against the ingrained self and the place and time of his birth. A quiet railing against the almighty Irish rubric of whatever you say say nothing – the title of one of his most political poems, whatever that is when its at home – and an equal reluctance to lift the megaphone for the Catholic minority held in the silent confinement of Stormont's sectarian state: "Where half of us, as in a wooden horse / Were cabin'd and confined like wily Greeks, / Besieged within the siege, whispering morse".

Heaney has not strayed far from the tribal Trojan Horse, yet he has never allowed himself to be press-ganged into storming the city gates either. He has held the line, cutting loose only behind the cloak of classical allusion lest he stir up the natives or set off the bear traps in Britain. Ever erring on the side of coziness, or the Olympian. All entirely understandable. Like Yeats he has been fearful of giving the gunslingers any more ammunition. Too fearful maybe.

His father was a cattle dealer and Heaney the poet has the same anxiety about his beasts coming home to haunt him. You can be too hesitant for your own good, and in this time of neurotic semi-ceasefires, Heaney appears to have discovered a new courage and with it a well-spring of childhood memories to draw on.

In 'Keeping Going', a poem about his brother Hugh, who farms their home place in Bellaghy, and his reaction to the shooting of a police reservist in the village, there is a rawness we haven't seen in Heaney for a long while. A teasing of his own taboos, a reckoning up, a willingness to confront hard truths in his own language:

> But you cannot make the dead walk or right wrong.
> I see you at the end of your tether sometimes,
> In the milking parlour, holding yourself up
> Between two cows until your turn goes past,
> Then coming to in the smell of dung again
> And wondering, is this all? As it was
> In the beginning, is now and shall be?

'The Errand', a masterly put-up of a poem, has the same new-found strength and independence, of striking out again:

> "On you go now! Run, son, like the devil
> And tell your mother to try
> To find me a bubble for the spirit level
> And a new knot for this tie".

But still he was glad, I know, when I stood my
                      ground,

Putting it up to him
With a smile that trumped his smile and his fool's
                      errand,

Waiting for the next move in the game.

The book is scattered with startling switches from childhood to middle age, turns of perspective that spin on a half line, real high-wire Heaney like the wonderful 'A Sofa in the Forties'. Weans playing trains with the settee while, unspoken, distant cattle trucks head for Auschwitz.

Tollund, setting of one of his greatest poems, is revisited post-ceasefire, where he concludes, in a neat twist of the old rebel song:

Ourselves again, free-
willed again, not bad.

Inevitably you begin to wonder if his best work, like Yeats's, is to come in middle age. That he will buy a tower with the Nobel loot and slip into the old boy's velvet tasselled slippers. People bang on about parallels, and they are there – both are men of inaction in troubled times, guarding their art from the pollution of the public. But they are very different animals. It's Paddy Kavanagh's hobnailed boots outside the back door we should be watching for.

Something was stirring in Heaney's last collection, *Seeing Things*. Awe and wonder. One-lunged Kavanagh was germinating, up and out of the grave again, eulogising dock leaves and nettles, small forgotten things. That same humility, suffused with the sacral is here again in the prayer quality of the opening poem 'The Rain Stick'. It is an invocation, the summoning of the inward spirit, a hue and cry

for the soul. Stop, it says, and listen:

You are like a rich man entering heaven
Through the ear of a raindrop. Listen now again.

Heaney has rescued a rain stick, one of those dusty lengths of hollow wood full of rice you find in the kitschy corners of New Age shops, way behind the cosmic crystals and essential oils, and used it as his evangelical's bell. The same second sight kicks through several other poems, most notably 'Mint' and the sublime 'Postscript'. The revelations don't end there. Heaney puts on his best gumshoe for 'The Flight Path', the IRA-Tried-To-Get-Me-To-Bomb-Pettigo-Border-Post poem, which has some great stuff about leaving home, and those who are left, a recurring motif in this collection. There is also his contrary peace-making with Hugh MacDiarmid, a telling little tribute if ever there was one.

'Mycenae Lookout' is back in Siege of Troy country, and is the longest and one of the most powerful poems in the collection, jacking up language and getting in underneath it, cannibalising old parts for the new chassis.

He still has his fetish for object poems and Buddha meditations on craft or profession that wind to a perfect chime, some more convincingly than others, but overall you get the feeling of greater daring, of heading in a new, older direction.

There has been a great deal of head-scratching over where this collection comes in the Heaney pantheon. It is very good. Better than there's been for a long time. We only have our expectation to measure it against. So the next may be the one to watch.

Book of Satin Phrases

by Sheenagh Pugh

EAVAN BOLAND
Collected Poems
Carcanet, £9.95,
ISBN 1 85754 220 7

THERE ARE SO many collections these days that one often doesn't become aware of a poet until he or she is well-established. First collections are not widely reviewed and it takes a rave notice to make you buy one. More often you get to know a poet who already has a style, but you've no idea how he/she developed it.

This was certainly true of me and Boland. I knew her from her last three books with Carcanet, and assumed from them that she was almost purely a free-verse poet – there would be the odd rhymed or half-rhymed poem, like 'Time and Violence', but mostly she didn't seem interested in shaping things.

She was once, though. Her first collection, published when she was 22, and which I'd never encountered, turns out to have been emphatically rhymed; so was what is in here of her second (incidentally, *is* a Collected Poems, or is it not, every published poem someone has written?). This one, unusually, has a preface, in which she says: "in the earliest work I was often too young, too puzzled, too clumsy as a technician to compose my intuitions into forms and therefore trapped them into patterns". This is true enough of some of the slightly stilted, heavily Yeats-influenced early poems, like 'The Poets':

> Just as the jewelled beast,
> That lion constellate,
> Whose scenery is Betelgeuse and Mars,
> Hunts without respite among fixed stars

(I do believe you have to turn that into a nineteenth-century "fixèd" to make it scan). It would be true of anyone who first published poems at 19. But presumably, as she grew older, she could have learned to make patterns serve her. It seems odd that she turned her back so firmly on them. Some of her free verse now is easy to defend from the charge of being prose in lines:

> Under low skies, past splashes of coltsfoot,
> I assumed
> the hard shyness of Atlantic light
> and the superstitious aura of hawthorn.
> ('White Hawthorn in the West of Ireland')

And some isn't:

> the nation, the city
> which fell
> for want of
> the elevation in
> this view of the Piazza
> ('Canaletto in the National Gallery of Ireland')

That's the kind of poem of which students ask: why are the line breaks *there,* rather than some other place; and you have the hardest time answering.

If those are the patterns, what are the "intuitions" she puts into them? In her early work she was heavily into mythology (there are still unexpectedly frequent classical allusions), though there were also poems about family, pets, animals (my own favourite being the zoo lion "bored as a socialite / With her morning post", who "slit / a rabbit open like an envelope" in 'Prisoners'). Ireland was always there, though more as an historical than a contemporary entity; witness her sequence on the Famine. And what might be described as the Role of the Poet came to be more important. But the word, above all, that keeps suggesting itself is "domestic". It isn't just the themes. The imagery too is preoccupied with the domestic, particularly fabric – outside John Lewis's you will never see quite so many materials. The "book of satin phrases" ('Beautiful Speech'); the fuchsia like "whitby jet fringing / an old rose printed shawl" ('Doorstep Kisses'); the "language that is lace" ('Lace'). And those are just the metaphors; the later poems especially are also full of materials in their own right – silk, wool, linen, crêpe, tulle, the black lace fan my mother gave me...

So what does that show? That this is a very tactile, sensual poet, dealing in the human rather than the abstract? That seems a reasonable conclusion – even when Big Ideas, like ageing and death, appear, they tend to be expressed this way:

I am perishing – on the edge and at the threshold of
the moment all nature fears and tends towards:
the stealing of the light. Ingenious facsimile.
And the kitchen bulb which beckons them
makes my child's shadow longer than my own.
('Moths')

In the end, though I admire her skill, she is not to my personal taste, because I find the insistent domestic ambience suffocating. People seem to be forever sanding floorboards, candle-greasing cupboard drawers, wrapping parcels or sewing. Maybe for some people, this *is* real experience, but surely it can't be true for many, particularly urban working women who don't have time to scent anything with lemon balm. Much of it relates to her mother's time, and I can't see it as very relevant to mine. This is personal, but to me, ideas often seem stifled under a weight of minutiae, as if under a pile of those fabrics. 'Parcels', where she describes her mother wrapping one, is, I think, about transience and loss. But by the time I'd read 30-odd lines of loving detail about the brown paper, the scissors, the twine, the luggage label, I was too bored by what felt like trivia to be moved. Maybe this sense of domestic claustrophobia is just what she's trying to achieve, in which case she succeeds, but for this reader there isn't much entertainment value in it.

Sheenagh Pugh's latest collection is *Sing for the Taxman* (Seren, 1993).

Tradition and the Individual Irish Talent

by Conor Kelly

THOMAS KINSELLA
The Dual Tradition:
An Essay on Poetry Politics in Ireland
Carcanet, £9.95,
ISBN 1 85754 182 0

From Centre City
Oxford University Press, £7.99,
ISBN 0 19 282272 1

GERALD DAWE
Against Piety: Essays in Irish Poetry
Lagan Press, £7.95,
ISBN 1 873687 75 3

False Faces: Poetry, Politics and Place
Lagan Press, £4.95,
ISBN 1 873687 20 6

Heart of Hearts
Gallery Press, £5.95,
ISBN 1 85235 153 5

BRENDAN KENNELLY
Poetry My Arse
Bloodaxe, £9.95,
ISBN 1 85224 323 6

EAMON GRENNAN
So It Goes
Gallery Press, £6.95,
ISBN 1 85235 170 5

"NO POET, NO artist of any art has his complete meaning alone. His significance, his appreciation is the appreciation of his relation to the dead poets and artists". These sentences, taken from T. S. Eliot's celebrated essay *Tradition and the Individual Talent*, have a haunting resonance for many contemporary Irish poets, including those under review, aware, as they are, of the imposing nature of a tortured literary and linguistic past.

Thomas Kinsella

Tradition, Eliot claims, "cannot be inherited, and if you want it you must obtain it by great labour". That labour is evident in Thomas Kinsella's criticism and poetry. His book-length essay, *The Dual Tradition*, is part of an immense labour of defining the role of the modern Irish poet against the tangled background of a tradition that is dual both in language and in politics. Aware that "Gaelic" and "Anglo-Irish" literatures are treated as separate traditions, it is Kinsella's view that Irish literature "exists as a dual entity . . . composed in two languages" and that a dual approach is "essential if the literature of the Irish tradition is to be fully understood". Domination and assimilation, in both language and politics, are seen as opposing polarities of a poetic tradition which Kinsella traces with diligence, enthusiasm and scholarship from the sixth to the twentieth century. He is particularly astute in dealing with the inadequacies of the nineteenth century poets and the "colonial impulse, to present the home literature to a 'senior' outside audience for its amusement and instruction". The contradictory roles of Yeats and Joyce in the dual tradition which Kinsella attempts to establish is cogently explored, even if the conclusion is a little too succinct: "Yeats stands for the Irish tradition as broken, and Joyce stands for it as healed – or healing – from its mutilation".

The book, however, has its weaknesses. What cannot be accommodated within the dual tradition is often redefined. To claim, as Kinsella does, that "Northern poetry is a journalistic entity rather than a literary one" is an understandable effort to poetically deny partition in Irish poetry. But it begs more questions of some of the finest Irish poets writing today than this lengthy intriguing essay can answer.

Politics, poetry and their traditional roles in Irish life are also the subject of Kinsella's own poetry which has often been animated by anger at the political, cultural, social, even poetical depredations of Irish life. At his best this anger gives his poems a red-hot intensity; at his weakest the anger exemplifies bile, vituperation and splenetic tirades. Sadly the poems in *From Centre City* rarely rise to his best practice. Aware of the problem, his long opening poem embraces squalor and satire, piling on the animus in an attack on unnamed poets, politicians, property developers, until it collapses, exhausted by its own anger:

Enough.
That there is more spleen
than good sense in all of this, I admit . . .

It is not the lack of good sense that vitiates many of the poems but the spleen. While there is no doubt that the anger is often justified on a personal level, it is not specified on a poetical level. Put this in Eliot's terms where "poetry is not a turning loose of emotion, but an escape from emotion" and it can be argued that the artistic escape is rarely effected. When the poems find an appropriate form for the seething emotions, when, "I found a structure for my mess of angers", then the lines are taut with tension. A variety of literary forms – satire, memoir, elegy, fantasy – are indulged in Kinsella's fragmented manner. There is even a down-beat, down-sized Dublin *Dunciad*, 'Open Court', that flickers into grim humour as it pulverises a few local poets. But sombre and self-contained as these poems may be, they are also, to this reader, oddly forbidding.

Gerald Dawe

A far more sympathetic account of Thomas Kinsella's poetry is offered by a younger poet and critic, Gerald Dawe, in separate essays in separate critical books. In *Against Piety,* the more scholarly and substantial collection of essays, Kinsella is celebrated for his "sense of an uncompromising artistic confrontation" and while Dawe is aware of the disdainful difficulties and experimental diffusions in some of the poetry, he is also aware of both the achievement ("incontrovertible truthfulness") and the influence ("He has flushed out the complacent poeticisms that obscure the language of poetry in Ireland by writing in an anti-eloquent diction . . .") which Kinsella continues to enjoy. Furthermore Dawe takes some of Kinsella's ideas on a "gapped, discontinuous, polyglot tradition" and develops them with a breath-taking ingenuity and appropriateness in two introductory essays on modern and contemporary Irish poetry. Many of the essays offer a sympathetic, yet studied account of individual Irish poets and their relationships with a complex, yet distinct sense of a tradition that is constantly being reworked.

Less intense, more personable, but no less exacting are the essays on poetry, politics and place collected in *False Faces*. This may be literary journalism, but it is journalism of the highest order. Arguing that "we have grown accustomed to narrow ways of reading poetry", Dawe explores in an incisive and intuitive manner what words like "home" and "exile" mean when applied to a variety of modern Irish and international poets. And this poetry is placed in a broad context. The title essay begins with a critical analysis, not of a poem, but of a newspaper photograph and skillfully goes on to deal with the manner in which popular Irish prejudices distort the reception of Michael Longley's poetry. Like Eliot, Dawe is aware that "poetry is not the expression of personality" and applies this awareness to the manner in which, in too much contemporary criticism, "the emphasis falls upon the personality of a poet rather than where it rightly belongs – with the poetry". His understanding of Irish poetry in particular and of its place in a changing political and social landscape is expressed with discrimination, judgement and a cogent and engaged style. "For the response of the individual imagination is born of the need to get through as best it can to whoever cares to listen".

Whoever cares to listen to Gerald Dawe's own poetry, particularly his new collection *Heart of Hearts*, will hear a quiet, elegant and eloquent voice which uses poetry to blow gently the dust off memories of what is absent, lost but not forgotten. "Who will ever remember that this was so? / I can hardly even hear my own footsteps". Hardly. But the poems do hear and do find a voice for what is often ignored: furtive and fugitive experiences rendered in an imagery that is both precise and evocative.

> They'll soon be forgotten about,
> like other things – the rusted hood
> of a pram; unopenable pots of paint.

Those unopenable pots of paint conceal what they contain. And the incisive images etched into these poems are rarely put to programmatic uses. There is an appealing openness to the aura of the experiences described and an unwillingness to dwell too insistently on what the images might be made to yield. "What this means I cannot say". While Kinsella may disdain as mere journalism the notion of a Northern tradition, these poems do share with other poets from the province a care for craft, an eye for the suggestive detail and a mind capable of making melody out of the mundane and the personal.

Brendan Kennelly

Another melody, another personality and another quite distinct Southern tradition is evident in the work of Brendan Kennelly who, according to one of Dawe's essays, is to contemporary Ireland what

Kavanagh was to the Republic of the '40s and '50s. "Both poets are haunted by bardic nostalgia; both are suspicious of high-brow pretensions about 'Art'; both are mindful of the subversiveness of the comic spirit and both respect the rhetorical wisdom of anecdote and folklore".

Kennelly's ambition in these directions has been clearly signalled over the past two decades in two previous epic poems, *Cromwell* and *The Book of Judas*, both extremely subversive of current trends in Irish poetry. As if to outdo these, *Poetry, My Arse* is a riotous epic poem with a riotous epic hero (Ace de Horner) which continually, over 500 distinct poems in over 350 pages, attempts to subvert the poet, the poem, the politics, the place and the pieties of a polite tradition. "Brown-tongued", his publisher calls it. And brown-tongued it certainly is. Yet it is arguably the least successful of Kennelly's epics, substituting the perverse for the poetic without earning the appropriate energy. ("Certain forms of energy leave everybody bored".) Or, as Eliot put it more incisively, "One error, in fact, of eccentricity in poetry is to seek for new human emotions to express; and in this search for novelty in the wrong place it discovers the perverse".

Eamon Grennan's

poems seek the old human emotions – loss, love, loneliness – and, rather than plunder tradition to express them, find a rich and ruminative form to explore their intricate enablings. They are marked by an intensity of clarity that is Wordsworthian in its natural piety. *So It Goes* is not only a title, but a treatment of experience as evanescent. The book is dominated by elegies – particularly for his parents – in which the loss is registered in lines of absorbing memory and introspection. Again and again the poems circle around the themes like hovering hawks (ornithology has long had an animating role in Grennan's poetry) as they work hard to convey the depths of their emotions: "there's neither going back nor going forward, only this / running in place as usual, trying to see more deeply in". At their best, and there are many good poems in this fourth collection, they see more deeply into "that silence that's the regional dialect of the dead". In charting that regional dialect while remaining open to the intricacies of the natural world – there is a remarkable poetic dissection of a firefly in one poem – Grennan allows us to see more deeply into a world he has made more resonant.

The Hour Between Dog and Wolf

by Deryn Rees-Jones

CAROL RUMENS
Best China Sky
Bloodaxe, £6.95,
ISBN 1 85224 337 6

IN HER PREFATORY note to *Thinking of Skins: New and Selected Poems* (Bloodaxe 1993), Carol Rumens spoke of an "uncertainty of location, this instability of ground beneath me (which feels so insistently like home) that is responsible for ... the lack of focus or the peculiar focus, in the work". Many of the poems in the new collection, *Best China Sky*, also stem, we are told, from her residency at Queen's, Belfast in the year following the ceasefire, and, throughout the three sections of the volume – 'Home Fires', 'Celtic Myths', and 'Learning to be Mortal' – Rumens continues to pursue a preoccupation with important and complex issues: language (and the loss of it) myth, love, desire, and not least, her relationship with Ireland.

If skin was the metaphor acting to resolve Rumens' interests in the earlier work, then it is the image of house which now figures most prominently as a trope for a whole series of juxtapositions and contradictions – stability and flux, inside and outside, the strange and the familiar. One of Rumens' important influences throughout the volume, both thematically and linguistically, seems to be Medbh McGuckian – who we perhaps hear echoes of in phrases such as "Your eyes were between-coloured / From the world of names" ('Literacy') or in 'Morning Card' where a window is described as "white and insatiable as a letter / With an unslept blackness round it". This influence is again apparent in 'A Cloud House', where she writes: "I'm only playing / At exile", continuing: "I'm disturbed by fixity / Yet wish there were no choice but to be fixed". But the poem is also dedicated to, and addressed to, the Elizabeth Bishop who describes herself in her letters at one point as "the loneliest person who ever lived", a quote which serves as the epigraph to the poem. Negotiating a sense of the

self through geography has been a recurrent theme in Rumens' work, so it's interesting to see her making the connection between the two (connections which are made through geography and the body in very different ways, for instance, in the work of Jo Shapcott). The poem is also one of the many in the collection which uses the window as a way of figuring difference, between poet, reader and poem:

> And what am I to you, fumbling about
> the sealed transparent window of a poem?
> No love can let me in or out.

In the title poem Rumens also uses the prism, "a sword-flash rainbow", as a metaphor for poetry:

> The prism comes and goes:
> Wonderful stain, transparency of art!
> A smoke-wraith sails right through it.
> But now it strengthens, glows and
>   braves its span,
> You'd think it was the rim
> Of some resplendent turquoise plate,
> Offering hills and cranes and streets
>   and us
> Fancies designed to melt
> As our fingers touched them.

David Hunter

So while windows and skin, each in their different ways, work as images of flux and in-betweenness, the prism serves as a image of transformation and transfiguration. Again in 'Windowscapes' we see a rainbow through a window as the snow keeps "fixing" and "dissolving".

It is this interest in the movement between the private and the public, the inner and the outer, the fluid and the solid, which is the distinguishing feature of Rumens' work. Very often her obliqueness acts as a lever rather than an obfuscation to truth, her ironic, often slippery use of language forcing us as reader to shift and renegotiate our position constantly. Sometimes this strategy can become difficult to the point of dissatisfaction. In 'Like It Is' Rumens supplies a note which reads that "the pronunciation of Blodeuwedd should be anglicised with a hard D in reading this poem. *Hiraeth* means grief". If she is making a point about the Anglicisation of, and mis-speaking of Welsh words, then why give us a meaning for *hiraeth* which means so much more than she is telling us? It's here that I feel that I am simply missing the point. Overall though – and perhaps this is the point – these are poems about process, and what is outstanding about Rumens' work is her willingness to concede her *own* bewilderment, her ability to write from an intrinsic sense of honesty about her feelings and the world, in a way that is unafraid of dealing with difficulty, which retains and maintains authority, but does not seek to control or administer 'truth'. As she writes in the 'Song of the Non-Existent':

> This is the wolf's hour, after all; he turns it between
> his teeth:
> The watery city thickens, blackens: all that the
> angels leave
> Is this: your sudden reluctance to remember
> How hard it was, and how beautiful to live.

IAN CAWS

IN WHICH A MOTORIST, WITH TIME AVAILABLE, STOPPED AT IPING AND REMEMBERED THE INVISIBLE MAN

When I stopped, not entirely for the rain,
I might have felt a compulsion fading
But for the card, there with the writing on,
And a time, though not of my deciding,
Waiting beyond the trees but before night.

Still, it would not always have been like this,
Though maybe, at last, we are all fiction
Like Griffin, who came here through an author's
Head and whatever fresh interaction
On the blank pages he could discover.

To be as invisible as the ghosts
In our children along by this stone bridge,
Though just as much perceived. And to part mists
By headstrong water crashing east, a smudge
Of wind turned calm when the rain stopped, later.

But mostly, it is truth that stays hidden
From us rather than the other way round.
So the rain bounced off my car and ran down
The lane. And grateful for a small thing found,
I opened the door and heard my footfall.

Felt the water define my face and legs
And caught the glance of a bustling woman,
Who, in the afternoon would pile more logs
On her lambent grate and forget a man
Who arrived early and was leaving late.

The Matter of Pain

by Jerzy Jarniewicz

Voices of Conscience.
Poetry from Oppression

Eds. Hume Cronyn, Richard McKane, Stephen Watts,
Iron Press, £12.99,
ISBN 0 906228 5 3

POETS HAVE LONG played two different, contrasting roles: they have been seen as dandified figures, detached from the mundane world, indifferent to the hardships and drab realities of everyday life. On the other hand, they have often been expected to represent the voice of conscience, to act as witnesses to history, or spokesmen for the oppressed. What one group considered a legitimate concern of poetry, the other tended to debase and discredit as detrimental to the very idea of literature. Politics seemed to be one such topic: at the same time that it is looked down upon as contingent, ephemeral, trivial, it has persisted in the work of great poets, from Homer, Dante, to Yeats and beyond.

Voices of Conscience gathers over 150 poets, writing in forty languages, all of whom record – as the editors note – "the experience of state-inflicted oppression and terror". This world-wide anthology of poems demonstrates an unprecedented historical survey, a history of twentieth-century atrocities, from the genocide in Armenia, the Holocaust, Communist tyranny, to the often veiled persecution of ethnic and sexual minorities, and the fate of women. Such a selection of poems implies that history and oppression are in fact synonymous. The poets offer horrifying testimony of our age, showing that although forms of oppression may change, the experience of pain inflicted and the keen sense of injustice are substantially the same in all times and in all places. The 150 poets, so different that it is impossible to imagine them sharing the same space in any other anthology, stand together here as dissenters against oppression.

Yet the power of this ambitious anthology is also its weakness. First, there is the question of defining oppression: while the majority of poems collected deal with obvious cases of state terrorism, persecutions, wars and purges, others simply record the authors' experiences in prison, irrespective of whether the charges were political or not. One

wonders whether it is appropriate to include Oscar Wilde's 'The Ballad of Reading Goal' in the same anthology that relates the account of the Holocaust. The question arises whether the editors have tried to suggest that oppression is an ahistorical phenomenon, characteristic of all political systems, including the so-called western democracies, and that the difference between them is only quantitative. This would be a gross misconception, as I think the editors would agree. I would rather assume that the anthology tries to show poetry in its public function, that of registering and detecting injustice in whatever form.

The arrangement of the anthology is not always convincing: it alternates between the chronological and the geographical. It is interesting that the only sections defined more specifically by historical periods (Fascism, The Holocaust, The Greek Civil War, Communism) relate to European history, whereas all the other sections are arranged only geographically, as if, for example, South America had no history of struggle with tyranny. It also is not always clear why the editors have decided to group poets in the way they have: why, for example, poems by Różewicz or Pilinsky are grouped under the heading 'European Communism: Post-1945', when all of them deal with the experience of the second world war and its aftermath.

And then, the book offers an odd selection of authors. Alongside poets who took up political issues openly, one finds authors who have always stood apart from political turmoil, such as, on the one hand, Oscar Wilde, and, on the other, Cavafy and Mandelstam. Some of them, it would seem, found their place in the anthology not so much through the political content of their work, as for the imprisonments, persecutions, or episodes of active political involvement in their biographies.

It is interesting that most of the poets included in the anthology spent years in prison, or were themselves victims of state oppression. The editors admit that they have tried to avoid over-emphasising the image of poet-as-victim, but when one reads in the notes that "he was never in prison" (Cavafy), "certainly he was not imprisoned by the regime" (Illyes), "she was neither imprisoned nor strictly speaking censored" (Nagy), "though never imprisoned he was undoubtedly harrassed and intimidated "(Vysotsky), one feels that apologetic excuses are being made for certain inclusions, as if imprisonment itself granted a poet the right to appear in the anthology. The danger of identifying pain with poetry has been observed by a Polish dissident poet, Stanislaw Baranczak, sadly not represented in the anthology. Baranczak in his short poem 'Never Really' (translated by Magnus J. Krynski and Robert A. Maguire) comments on the sad irony and moral ambivalence of the situation that is confronted by poets writing under oppression:

I never really felt the cold, never
was devoured by lice, never knew
true hunger, humiliation, fear for my life:

at times I wonder whether I have any right to write.

Jerzy Jarniewicz teaches at the University of Łódź, Poland.

Contending and Cohering

by Neil Powell

MICHAEL HAMBURGER
Collected Poems 1941–1994

Anvil Press Poetry, £25.00,
ISBN 0 85646 266 7

IN 1959, PHILIP LARKIN wrote to his old friend Robert Conquest, who was about to commence a year's fellowship at the University of Buffalo, imagining the kind of question he might expect from his students: "Wud you mind giving us your opinion of the relative indebtedness to William Blake and, say, Hölderlin, of Mr Michael Hamburger, Professor Conquest?" It's a typically sour and self-mocking bit of little-Englandism, and (also typically) it makes an unnervingly accurate point; for the monolingual English reader may well find himself in resentful awe of the polyglot poet and translator, whose ability to range across European cultures might seem almost like cheating.

Hamburger is a poet of contending and ultimately cohering dualities – German-Jewish and English, urban and rural, didactic and meditative. In a crucially self-defining poem called 'The Dual Site', which dates from 1955, he addresses his alter ego, "my twin who lives in a cruel country", who in turn replies that beyond the "tangle" of their mutual anxieties lies "the dual site / Where even you and I / Still may meet again and together build / One house before we die". This is the reconciliation at last achieved by these *Collected Poems*, but the journey they record is a long and uncomfortable one. It begins impressively if fairly conventionally: Hamburger published his first collection at the age

of twenty-one, and the few poems he has allowed to survive from this and his next two books range from a suitably bold weather-and-landscape sonnet, 'November' ("I have watched the hypocritical dawn / and the murderous dusk daubed with lavish hands / on the daily sky ..."), to an ambitious sequence, 'From the Notebook of a European Tramp', which draws, as he explains in a preface, on his "experiences as a soldier, not a tramp, in post-war Europe". This "Author's Note", incidentally, seems finicky and mildly obstructive – as such things so often are – and leaves the reader perversely wanting to track down the excluded poems.

In some of his poems of the 1950s, Hamburger trades his youthful descriptive vigour for a universality which can look rather pallid and deracinated: when, in 'An Unnecessary Visit', he describes himself as "Like one on a pub-crawl in a foreign city" and finds he's in hell, it seems a logical enough step from a somewhat austere post-war urban world. On country matters, however, his voice is warmer and surer. In 'A Horse's Eye', the occasion suggests Ted Hughes and the tone Edward Thomas, but the affectionate yet unsentimental meditative stance is all Hamburger's own:

I did not stop today at the five-barred gate,
Did not wait for the old white draught-horse at grass,
Unshod, unharnessed these many years; walked past,
Preoccupied, but something made me look back:
Her head was over the gate, her neck was straight,
But I caught her eye, a wicked, reproachful look
From one small eye slanted in my direction.

Unaffected, almost under-written, this opening has the notebook-accuracy and the deceptively modest integrity which distinguishes much of his later work.

The problem – if that's the right word – in the middle of this fine book stems from a quite different sort of poem, which Hamburger himself admits has been "disliked by my readers, if not totally ignored": these are the 'Unpleasantries', many of them deriving from his visits to America in the late 1960s and early 1970s. 'Newspaper Story', a fair rather than an extreme example, recounts the tale of Gary from Hartford City, Indiana, with hair of "un-American length" who, lacking a house or indeed a flagpole, with apparently patriotic intent pinned up the US flag as a curtain in his minibus and for this act of desecration "was sentenced to bear / Old Glory for three hours / Outside the City Hall": the anec-dote is well-told and effectively detailed, but the point is too insistently hammered home. Ironically, this poem – like others in the same section – closely resembles the furiously didactic pieces written at the same time by Donald Davie, then also teaching in America but self-exiled from an England he had found politically intolerable: Hamburger's stance may be more obviously sympathetic, but the prob-lem of converting angry polemic into effective poetry remains intractable in each case.

After this troubled and troubling patch, the later poems chart a prolific and increasingly relaxed course of renewal and regeneration: they include two sets of 'Variations' ('Travelling' and 'In Suffolk'); the continuing, beautifully observed and botanically informed 'Tree Poems'; and, by no means least, a number of short pieces collected here for the first time. It's in some of these quite recent poems that I find Hamburger's earlier tensions most convincingly resolved: here letters to literary friends and conversations with rural codgers (and even with a blackbird) share a common tone of civilised attentiveness; extended postcards from Salzburg and Stuttgart show the same care for detail as the seasonal jottings from his Suffolk garden. It's an entirely convincing synthesis of art and life, achieved through great resilience, rather as the neglected roses which he notices at an unmanned railway halt "by defiance have proved themselves / The nature they never were". One could, without being completely ridiculous, say that something of the sort is what poetry is all about.

Esh

by Keith Jebb

DOUGLAS OLIVER
Penniless Politics
Bloodaxe, 1994, £7.95,
ISBN 1 85224 269 8

"What was the shock like, reading T. S. Eliot's *The Waste Land* when it was first published in 1922? I think I know. I've just read Douglas Oliver's epoch-making long poem, *Penniless Politics*. I never thought I should read anything like it in the 1990s. *Penniless Politics* sets the literary agenda for the next 20 years."
    – Howard Brenton, Foreword to *Penniless Politics*

WHAT A SOD advertising is. The above originally appeared in a review of the first publication of the poem (in 1991 by Iain Sinclair's Hoarse Commerce press) in the *Guardian* on 7 April 1992. The whole of this review is printed as the foreword here by Bloodaxe, a context in which it reads like a eulogy, not only that, but a self-serving eulogy, something I'm sure a poet of Oliver's integrity would not want.

The problem with such a set-up, of course, is that if you disagree with the eulogy, it will appear that you will be running the poem down. I don't, and I'm not. Perhaps in 1922 there was a reviewer who wrote "I now know what a shock it was to read *In Memoriam* when it was first published". No, *Penniless Politics* doesn't "set the literary agenda for the next 20 years". We can let the next 20 years work that one out. But it should surely take an idiot or a chauvinist not to see that a singular literary agenda is not going to emerge from a multicultural English language writing scene; and a look at the pluralistic strategies of *Penniless Politics* itself should have made it obvious. Oliver is acutely aware in the poem of his subject position as a white European middle-class middle-aged poet, setting his poem in a predominantly African American area of New York, where he lived at the time that it was written. The poem in fact contains its own male white poet, Will, who writes the poems of the multicultural revolution which is the poem's own story. It is a gesture in which Oliver attempts to contain himself (more in the limiting, rather than the inclusive sense) within his own writing:

Their poet has a white male face just as mean as each
face
of rich white males in today's *Post*: the New York
Mayor race.

So though he may tell he may not star in the story,
                                                outlawed
from penniless power. He (Will) tells how that day,
                                                bored ...

This is perhaps more than just a PC gesture, though it is that as well. It also sets up a tone for the manipulation of the poem by the poet, the way it is aware that its utopianism is never more than just that; that the nonviolent, resourceful, trickster-like (non)political party of the piece, Spirit, is just spirit. So he can round on the reader in the end:

All too soon Spirit seemed to have aged.
As it does: it can never breathe for more than a
                                                moment before
a poem is finished. What did you expect? You,
                                                hypocrite reader,
et cetera? You want some opiate, a poetic abracadabra
so your ordinary responsibility for our ordinary
                                                political failure
can be charmed away?

Between these two gestures, Oliver narrates the gesture of Spirit, which, by a combination of Voodoo and publicity stunt, galvanises a diverse population into forms of more or less spontaneous collectivism, writes its own version and amendment of the Constitution and secedes from the United States: except that District A1 as they call it is so mysterious, the authorities cannot find it to see if the secession is real.

The poem appropriates Voodoo spirituality, not the clichéd world of pinned dolls and exotic dancing but the spirit-possession by a loa, or rider, of Emen, Will's African-American partner. The loa utilises a multilingual punning speech which helps to establish some of the sexual politics of the poem, using the pronoun *esh*, "a nimble she in reverse", taking its power to be the female transcending the female. This is not unproblematic. But none of this poem is. Even the counterpoint of a tight economic prose style marshalled into rhyme is almost designed to raise questions. The cumulative effect is very different for instance, from the virtuosity of his brilliant *The Infant and the Pearl* (1985).

But it engages with Oliver's abiding concerns about the extent to which politics in its widest sense is predicated on harm, familiar in his *three variations on a theme of harm* (Paladin, 1990) which includes *The Infant and the Pearl*. Spirit's non-violence is compromised by the fact that High John, its most innocent activist and major financial benefactor, is a world champion boxer, combining the opposition between violence and childlike harmlessness which is the dialectic of the earlier volume. It is Oliver's agenda, an agenda that has its own naiveties, and its own value. It also has its ironies and sophistications.

Keith Jebb's study of Housman was published by Seren in 1992.

Stroke City

by Elizabeth Lowry

RUTH PADEL
Fusewire
Chatto, £6.99,
ISBN 0 7011 6379 8

IN RECOGNITION, PERHAPS, of an annoying obscurity in *Summer Snow* (Hutchinson, 1990) and *Angel* (Bloodaxe, 1993), the publisher's blurb for *Fusewire* promises that Ruth Padel's third collection "moves into new territory and new clarity". This is both true and untrue. Padel's poetry is still elliptical and crowded with private references,

although her enthusiasm for recondite vocabulary ("capybara", "sarsen" and "ophiclide" are just three examples from *Angel*) and the almost wilful hermeticism of some of the earlier pieces have on the whole been kept in check. The book picks up the erotic and political themes of her previous volumes and startlingly confirms the impression given there of a voracious imagination which finds its natural expression in a figurative language made up in equal parts of the appetitive and animal. Readers of *Summer Snow* will already be familiar with Padel's gastronomic similes, which have included curiosities such as "fudge-brown clouds", a "chocolate stoat", an "oatmeal sky" and a "coffee-icing cow". In *Fusewire* the human male is usually feral, "mischievous as a mongoose", a pelted creature about to "earth" his "way / into sleep", or more bluntly apostrophized ("you skelter away, closing your fur") as an arctic fox; while food is abundantly used to describe moments of arousal. A woman's hand is held between her lover's "like the filling in a sandwich"; in 'The Appointment' Elizabeth I is seduced by Raleigh's "Devon-cream brogue" and "malt eyes", and elsewhere the menu includes burnt Melba toast, strawberries, wild raspberries, honey, Australian Sauterne, and a glittering list of cocktails: Sierra Tequila, Ouzo Olympia, Albanian Kristal, Bull's Blood Glamorgan, Crème de Cacao de Campagne.

If the book finally fails it is because the poems are too often torn between this honest sensuality and a high moral seriousness. Padel has already proved her interest in global politics and the cultural effects of colonialism: *Summer Snow* concentrated on Venetian and Turkish expansion in Crete and Salonika, while *Angel* took in the Gulf, India, and Russia. Now the scene has shifted to Bosnia and Northern Ireland (this, presumably, is the "new territory" alluded to on the back cover). The Irish poems are lavishly supported by endnotes which fill in the gaps with historical quotations and authorial asides – turning to the notes for light on 'The Biggest Footprint', for instance, we are told that "it has been argued that the British relation to Ireland was not true colonisation. If that's right, this poem is less relevant than I thought". The bid for relevance is really part of the problem: the least successful of these pieces, the rhetorical 'Foreign News' and 'Stroke City', try too hard for significance. The best are playfully sardonic: 'Letter', describing the fortification of Derry by Monro ("such reeling times"), and the witty 'Your Place or Mine?', in which the clichéd sexual invitation doubles as a metaphor for English expansion in Ulster. The metaphorical interchangeability of sex and politics is itself of course by now a venerable cliché, which the poem introduces with true postmodernist aplomb. The volume's centrepiece, 'Desire Paths of Sarajevo', would have gained from a similar lightness of touch. Voiced for the poet, it is a tale of two cities narrated from the security of her lover's flat in Heraklion (an area which, according to the notes, "was colonised by Turkey for many centuries: like Sarajevo"). By way of comparison we are shown two Bosnian lovers whose biographies are introduced in potted form – he is a young doctor 'with a research interest in Indo-Chinese diseases ("He'd been on the trail / of phibellasomes in the immune system"); she is scarred on the thigh by a

shell ("He'd sewn it – / an Oxfam needle – but rarely saw it. / / Only in half hours off / the amputating table"). Transferred to Mostar, Dr. Phibellasome remembers the last night with his girl in Sarajevo:

> The night Sekakovic
>
> told General Kikanjac
> Go fuck himself
> or he'd blow the hydro-electric plant
> sky-high over Visegrad.
>
> The night they knew
> things had got mad. No backturn.
> And he'd knelt above her, parting her,
> two hands in a soft karate chop.

The casual obscenity of the poem's swaggering political commentary makes the martial sexual detail seem absurd instead of tender. Worse still, the contrast between the respective fates of the two cities is driven home with a little consumer information: in Heraklion the couple next door "argue in whispers / over nappies unavailable / in Sarajevo". Padel contrives the rhyme needed to continue this line of thought in the next stanza: "If *this* was Mostar? / / Maybe I've got it wrong. None of us are . . ." – perfect? That would be trite. Safe? Some of us are certainly safer than others. Her careless sleight of hand here disappoints precisely because she is so concisely evocative elsewhere: one thinks of the Royal Lancashire recruit perfecting his "lynx-in-kidboots shuffle" in 'Arctic Fox', or the kitsch "choc-ice Volvo" belonging to the Loyalist paramilitary in 'Tropicals', or the searingly brief moments of contact,

> in dark summer traffic
> and gunmetal Gothic
> Church of Ireland shade,

between the lovers in 'Sambuca'. *Gunmetal Gothic*: those two words say more about the cultural and political ambiance of Protestant Ulster, its garrison outlook and die-hard conservatism, than the whole of 'Desire Paths of Sarajevo' says about Bosnia – and there isn't a phibellasome in sight.

Elizabeth Lowry is deputy editor of *Thumbscrew* and writes for the *TLS*.

MARGARET SPEAK
THE FIREFLY CAGE

I carry the firefly cage
a calligraphy of willow
scribed into shape;
search among the stalks
of mangrove and bamboo
tease out the fireflies,
lifting them tenderly
stroking the dark lacquer shells.
Our dead Emperors brood
over us, their white caps
peaked with snow.

I have watched the fireflies:
the female sits on her elevated perch
the male times his signal
executes his exotic lantern pavan.
They meet and mate
their lights synchronise.
Sometimes a female impostor
makes fraudulent response.
I have found her devouring
his flesh; his light glows,
her light is carnivorous-bright.

My Master leads me into
the garden beyond the pagoda,
the sky washed pale as wisteria.
I carry the firefly cage,
loop it onto a branch of camellia.
We are caught in its halo
a leaf is detached by my clumsiness;
he shudders, sees images of death.
He is grave, I am solemn; he unpins
my black hair, unwinds
the sash of my kimono.
We sway in a hammock of night air
the cool moss embraces us.
We are drenched in a hoop of light,
a constellation of fireflies.

CLARE POLLARD
DREAM OF EXPLOSIONS

This is not feverish flamenco fire
Devouring my home like a loaf –
This is a margarine candle flame.
Enough light to read by.

This is not a black hole. Nothingness
So intense it thirsts for me –
This is a vacuum flask
Full of tea for two.

This is not drowning. Becoming a terrible bird
As the ocean vomits into me –
This is a soothing lukewarm bath
To cure my aching joints.

This is not an earthquake. The world's old wounds
Torn open again, like a bad case of scurvy –
This is the peel torn from a tangerine.
A good dose of vitamin C.

I am the cat that got the milk.
Woman who awoke in a warm bed
On a black-ice morning, and never got up again.
My life is nice. I raise a mild smile.

Yes, I dream of explosions
That shake my bones loose,
But what if this is the most violent?
What if this is it, my childhood dream?

I cannot let it go for a whiff of gunpowder.
If I stand in a lonely, open field
Trying to catch lightning bolts,
Perhaps I'll only catch my death of cold.

Oh, but if I caught that bolt
And sparked the world bulb bright!
Should I settle for this current
That keeps my TV running, but little more?

NEIL ROLLINSON
FREE FALL

His parachute felt like a satchel
of bricks on his back, he imagined
the canopy furled inside, every crease
and fold in the fabric critical, the rip-cord
beat on his chest like a metronome.
He couldn't get her face out of his mind.
I love you, he thought, I can't let you
watch me rot in a chair.
He was God for a moment, all the fields
and towns laid at his fingertips.
He could hear the plane as it moved away,
then just the rushing of air in his head.
He felt the disease creep through his legs.
As he fell through the sky he could smell
each tree, each of the hundred wild flowers
of Berkshire, the clean, damp scent of salmon
cruising the Thames. He fell through the blue
morning, slicing the endless half distances
he'd read about (a falling ball never reaches
the floor they say: he'd soon find out).
He thought about the bills he'd left,
the Minibels growing sweet in the greenhouse,
his wife's beautiful sad face; he fingered
the rip-cord, thought about pulling, there was
still time, just, but he'd made up his mind.
He remembered Gypsy Lee on their honeymoon
tracing the deep, unbroken life-line
round his thumb: a long, and happy life,
she'd said. The world turned green
as he travelled into the lawn of a council
house in Newbury, his mind so fast
he noticed the microscopic details of everything:
the point of a grass blade, the spores
of a mushroom, the head of a garden ant,
he could see his face in the hundred
facets of its eye as he fell through the roots
of dandelions, buttercups, and the muddy spirals
of worm-holes.

TOBIAS HILL

FROM: FOUR WAYS TO NAME THE CITY

1. What the City Says

Out to the bedroom-towns with their
lurch of headlights over sleeping policemen

goes the twelve-ten with half-empty seats
smelling of cigarettes and factories.

This is the dark between stations where
nobody talks to no-one and the river

looms like a high-rise
under piers and viaducts.

In the night train's public places
we are the photofit faces

watching closing-times and derelicts
out of windows puzzled with rain.

In transit nothing counts. It makes us
full of possibilities:

some of us dream of rush-hours,
some of us will be dangerous.
This is what we come to when

the overtime is gone and there is
nothing left to do but listen
for public announcements or aggression –

the voice into a cordless phone
that lies like a dentist to its loved one,

the movement of air
in tunnels and wires,

the track, which says
I am correct –
I am the click of binary
in satellite and sea-bed lines,
I am the atom in the clock
I am the metric length of gold.
It could be you. It could be you. It could
– and from the yards outside,

gently, the hush of a city and a river,
and the smell of rain coming in
through open doors at platforms and
                                        destinations.

WAYNE BURROWS
WOUNDED KNEE

The plastic raft's imitation logs and twine
Carry three Red Indians, wearing beads and suede,
Over difficult rapids conjectured from
Their kneeling postures and straining arms,
And a Chief, standing upright, in ceremonial dress
With a tomahawk held to his musclebound chest,
Who barks out orders like an Oxbridge cox.

They slide past jelly, pink salmon and crisps,
Past a giant, scuffed Action Man, sprawled out prone
(After sex with my sister's Sindy – again),
Past the Tabby-Cat Mountain, curled fast asleep
At the edge of the table on a red-checked cloth,
Past salt-pots, lettuce, bundled knives and forks,
Rolled pastry, tea-cups, and plates of cakes,

Till they come to a Chocolate-Finger stockade
Where the Cavalry crouch, with their rifles aimed,
Bogged down in a sticky, fast-setting cream.
The Indians halt, and hold their breaths,
Before they lunge at the raised Confederate flag
And a gigantic hand, wearing one gold ring,
Snatches them up through the air, and shouts –

For Christ's sake, can't you play somewhere else?
Next thing they know, they've hit the floor
And lie around scattered on its washed, red tiles,
Their postures frozen, their paddles lost,
Their raft buggered-off-with by a curious dog
That imprints its toothmarks into every log
Before proceeding to leg it, myself in pursuit.

Two weeks later, the raft's found beached,
Its whole crew missing, in the jaws of a sphinx
As it chews the last corner, looks up, bored,
Then skulks from the house to pester cats in the yard.
The Braves kneel forgotten by a potted plant
When their Chief is discovered with a plastic pig,
Conspiring to block up the Hoover-bag.

ROGER CRAWFORD
MA OLD SCHOOL FRIEND

for Mike Taylor

Aggie Macbeth rang up taeday;
She seemed agley – she seemed upset,
Even for hame the weather was grey
The cellars were dry and Glamis was wet.
Och, it's no much fun being merely a wife
When you're facing up tae the change o' life!

The servant problem's here tae stay –
What use are drunken porters, hen?
The rain, it raineth every day;
The ghosties been around again;
She said the Man was one big moan
And talked in his sleep of the Stone of Scone.

I said, puir dear, don' fash yoursel'.
Is there any wee favour I can do?
Macbeth should pull his weight – I ken
You do the worriting for two
(Och, it's no good enough for a bairnless wife
When she's facing up tae the change of life!)

And Duncan picky at his meal;
Demanding quail and sturgeon's roe!
(Of course he's king, but I always feel
In Rome you should do as the Romans do;
And the Macs like haggis and such things –
A fit – if filthy – dish for Kings.)

I thought she said she'd done some crimes
And Birnam'd come tae Dunsinane...
(The line tae Scotland's bad at times)
I think, tae be frank, she's a wee insane...
But it's no much fun being merely a wife
When you're facing up tae the change o' life!

GWYNETH LEWIS
PERIPHERAL VISIONS

1.

Not everyone sees the man inside the dog

I know him. Coming from the Harlequin's
after his snuffle through leaves in the lane
for a second he stood back to let me in

through the gate, so courtly that, on my inner eye,
I saw him for the first time clearly
not Staffordshire Bull, but a man in soft chamois,

tall like a prince, with thigh-length boots.
I said I would marry him. Sepia street lights
were our veil as I opened recalcitrant locks,

went in. This royal love needs no return
but the favours of fondle, hock bone, a run
through piss-scented parks in the afternoons.

As I hung up his lead, he was back on all fours,
wagging his tail by the kitchen door.
Beauty hides in the beast. This is the law.

2.

The gods are still walking around South Wales

In the paper, I read, a girl called on Apollo
not knowing it, outside the Monico
cinema, car idling. Stranger steps in. "We'll go

up to the Beacons", he said. "I am
the answer to your prayers, a dangerous man,
not *deus ex machina* but lunatic in van".

So she drove, directed by his Stanley knife,
fearing now for her hairdresser life,
on B roads, till he'd ravished her enough

in lay-bys and by picnic-area streams
to satisfy her carnap dreams.
They say she made it all up. But how come

her joy, despite all the names she was called
by cops and by journos? How come she recalled
a transport of love in a shower of gold?

3.

She dreams of the Prince of Frogs

I lower myself into my coffin bath
and lie there, thinking about my death
and whiteness. Suddenly my breath's

transformed by hag who, just for sport,
has placed toad pulses at ankle and throat.
The coming prince is a threat. But bodies float.

4.

Turn left at the supermarket and you're nearly there

Quick swerve and I'm at the experimental junction,
empty of traffic. A jenny hums
to make streetlight over this incarnation

of cones round a corner, this new way of turn-
ing quickly without coming to harm.
The motor roars like a poem and the cherubim

and seraphim of travel bear witness to the rout
of traffic lights for roundabout.
All praise to free will! All praise the grace of roundabouts!

5.

View from the poop deck of an ocean-going liner

Of *course* the great Spanish poet Juan Ramón
Jiménez saw the sirens as they sank
just off the coast of America. He sought

them for ever after, using the eye
that sees round the corners of things, that heeds
the flanks that flex in higher frequencies

than dust and daylight. Mostly he stayed stumm
about what he saw. But their lovely limbs
were a fact. They would be back to sing for him.

MATTHEW SWEENEY
CROSSING

He rode his horse into the sea and kept heeling it on.
The horse wasn't used to this, but proceeded to swim –
not easy, with the man and those wet jeans on its back –
but it made headway, out into the currents of the Channel
among the yachts, the windsurfers, the long-distance swimmers.
When the Caen to Portsmouth ferry passed, the Captain hooted.
The horse ignored this; the man took off his cap and waved.
Applause broke out among those few passengers on deck.
The man bowed his head into the sea and downed a mouthful.
He spat this out, then spoke for the first time to the horse
whose hooves kept flailing the water, swatting a few lobsters,
alarming squid, missing a frogman by centimetres.
The horse's head was higher now. Had it seen the Isle of Wight?
The man leant down and whispered promises in its ear –
once they hit land, a big bag of oats, a bigger bowl of cider.
He told it that no other horse had made this crossing,
and that once was enough – they'd take the ferry home.
The horse neighed as they passed a rock where a lighthouse
had just switched on, as if they both were expected,
and flashbulbs were ready on the beach, a studfarm waiting.

MAUREEN MACNAUGHTAN
OPEN LOTTERY

*"I feel that every country is entitled to it without any question of its
fitness or otherwise. As every country is fit to eat, to drink and to
breathe, even so is every nation fit to manage its own affairs, no
matter how badly... The doctrine of fitness to govern is a mere
eyewash. Independence means nothing more or less than getting out
of alien control" – Mahatma Gandhi, 1931*

Ever since the oil left
There's been a new revolution.
For quite a modest sum
Which includes the waterfalls
Skiing rights for the glen
And an outdoor slaughterhouse,
You can join the untouchables.

We have become a bazaar
For a few annual hawkers
And a never-ending fog.
Only the tied remain
To inspect the pot-holes
And serve the occasional guest.

Instead of the usual exchange rate,
For quite a modest sum
Which includes the best technology
From the most exported nation
We could stretch out –
Whistle, and close the bidding.

TWO POEMS BY DONALD DAVIE
THOMAS AND EMMA

Not deaf to ghosts yet not expecting them
I paced the hill-rim's shadowy belvedere
At Shaftesbury, when from the abbey ruins
An old thin voice pronounced, for me to hear:

"A levelled, levelling culture leaves no room
For amorous or other compliment.
Analogy and allusion are ruled out;
Our happiness can have no monument".

A voice returned: "The happiness alleged
To have obtained between us never was,
Or else so seldom that a truthful culture
Rightly discounts hyperboles like yours".

In the event I heard both voices falter.
Hyperbole, analogy, allusion
Build up what is no lie, although so wishful:
Conspiratorial, conjugal collusion.

This, though unsettled, was a summer's day –
I took another turn along the grass
And gravel of the rampart. Overhead
The boughs soughed something. It was not: "Alas".

TOBY TO AGUECHEEK

My mountain belly and incontinent girth
That strutted, more than trod, the groaning earth

Have, in some questionings of saluted merit
Worried that sheer bulk balks the encroaching spirit.

Carnality. But we worship the Incarnate:
Buried in the ageing flesh, or blossoming in it?

I who cull those blossoms know the truth:
Gross age engrosses all we risked in youth.

A fat man is as like to be a saint
As any hermit skeletal in paint,

I tell myself, and with more confidence
Now, in advanced age, needing her carnal presence

Whom no, my lean fastidious friend, you have
Not so much as entertained a thought of.

TIM LIARDET
DEATH'S SURROGATE DRESSES

The wardrobe is full of shaking bulbous light, a window
Of sky and summer cirrus because it has no back or front;
Inside it, a rail of summer dresses is flapping, flapping:
Eggshell-blue, vermilion, plum, scarlet and diaphanous,

As their hangers click and squeak the dresses lightly dance
Upon a dry airy wind that blows them through their choices,
Their inner seams in the sun a flow-diagram of dark.
Upon them all the very faintest fragrance of woman;

From their hems, a few stray strands of cotton blow . . .
A mind, through the early morning dream, surfaces
Like a grumbling official already become impatient
With colour and air and space, the subliminal stuff:

Deprived of its caffeic fix, begrudging of airspace, it
Fingers its way through the hangers mumbling: *frocks*.
It wishes in its upshuttering market to know who'll
Clear the job-lot for trading, gatecrashing meaning.

It lifts looking for a clue the one still attached price-tag
And like the mind it is seeks to sleuth a name out of the light
And is not satisfied at all. Quite in spite of it, I wake
With a warm wind and dress hems blowing in my smiling face.

CATE PARISH
JELLYFISH

We're jellyfish, just jellyfish
drifting in the waters of the Sound

We go here, or there,
we don't care,
the water moves us round

How could we know, we couldn't see
their boat go upside-down
It wasn't us, it was the sea
that made them run aground

on the island that said,
"Danger! Biological Warfare Experimentation Zone!
Keep Away!"

A little trance, a little wreck
surprising how little it takes
A little germ, a litte shock –
their minds become unsound.

Their minds unhinged,
we were aliens
come down to take them away
Yes, we were tentacled, gelatinous aliens
and we stunned them and whisked them away

To the Mother Ship, in the sky up above
where we applied our suction cups and feelers
and they struggled to perceive in this a higher form of love
and not just an experiment in cross-breeding.

But how misleading.

We're jellyfish, just jellyfish
drifting in the waters of the Sound

We go here, or there,
we don't care,
the water moves us round

And what are they?
We don't know.
They dreamed and then they drowned.

ARVIND KRISHNA MEHROTRA
MEMORANDA

The milk's delivered at six o'clock.
Try nature cure for writer's block.

Travel north in a southbound train,
And cross the desert on the wheels of rain.

Unload the boats anchored in the bay.
Deepen the channel, dredge out the clay.

Once the hum stops there's nothing you can do.
Your best lines those that didn't come through.

Tongue-tied at times, at times colour-blind,
Go fishing, then. There's nothing wrong with your mind.

View the passing show with an inward eye.
The average man is only five feet high.

Art is long, who doesn't know that.
Keep pedalling, friend, though the tyre's flat.

If not this, the next mile of verses
Could be the *annus mirabilis*.

TWO POEMS BY ALISTAIR ELLIOT

for J. M.

ON THE LAST DAY OF 1993

You gave me the beautiful
notebook. It is like a bowl
a helping of food would spoil.

I guess you couldn't bear to write
on its rag pages. It was uncut
and I guess you managed to open it,

but were overcome by its perfection.
It looks finished now. I shall have to begin
by mis-spelling my name on page 1,

and then more gently persevere
word by word, smear by smear,
till it's worn, obscure, and dear.

But it chose a good year to come:
In spring I sail to Byzantium.

FINISHING THE NOTEBOOK

Jimmy, two years ago you gave me this
notebook; and now I could return it full
you're dead, and writing to you is unreal.
I am addressing yesterday's clouds, for business
goes on without you.
                            But your new book came,
as if to tease me: I'll be in a file
on somebody's computer, and I smile
suddenly seeing you can play the game
one-sidedly – as when you were alive
in fact – with poems hidden in your shroud
generously sent, old love-codes read aloud
for the first time to old friends who survive.
And we can't answer, with applause or hisses:
your poems get better and better; we can't be heard,
but you keep on pronouncing a fresh last word.
We are reduced to blowing the wind kisses.

Laying Down the Law

by Justin Quinn

ANTHONY HECHT
On the Laws of the Poetic Art

The A. W. Mellon Lectures in the Fine Arts, 1992,
The National Gallery of Art, Washington, D.C.,
Princeton University Press, Bollingen Series XXXV: 41, 1995,
£19.95, ISBN 0 691 04363 9

IN THE PREFACE to *On the Laws of the Poetic Art* Anthony Hecht makes his apologies. Lots of them. Many are typical of those books whose chapters began life as lectures – and then there's a few more. It is strange to pick up a book whose title and appearance seem so certain of themselves in that old lost Aristotelian way, only to be assailed by such incontinent humility in its preface. Bemused by these conflicting messages, I decided to be ingratiated by Hecht's enumeration of the book's faults. Unfortunately, coming back to the preface again after having read the entire book, I simply nodded in disappointed agreement.

For in the three years between lecture series and publication Hecht himself seems to have realised a good deal about what's wrong with his book. Tongue-tied at all the wrong moments by politeness, eschewing any attempt to develop arguments while maintaining the semblance of Ciceronian consistency, this book lurches from one chapter to the next with neither rhyme nor reason. And within the chapters themselves Hecht relies on tenuous connections and anecdotes to keep up the momentum. Take 'Poetry and Music' for example. After recounting Stravinsky's amusing comments on Wagner, he tells another anecdote about how Piero della Francesca's revolutionary insights were plagiarised by his student (shouldn't this, we wonder, have gone in the chapter, 'Poetry and Art'?). Then he evokes the old chestnut that "numbers underlie the structure of the entire cosmos and all its motions", which, we take it, is a vague affirmation of time-honoured forms in both the musical and poetic arts. Rather than develop this highly questionable point, Hecht goes skating off in different directions – the Book of Job, Thomas Campion, Leonardo da Vinci, Joseph Haydn – to find the same idea expressed in different ways.

Granted, these digressions never fail to be interesting, but one has the niggling sense, as one is yet again dragged off, say, to consider the ground plan of Palladio's Villa Foscari, that this is leading nowhere. Why the excursion to Italy? To demonstrate how, if you juggle Palladio's proportions you end up with the ratio 8:6, which is, eureka, that of the Petrarchan sonnet. Which is in turn, I suppose, meant to bring us back to the idea that numbers underlie everything. If this counts as Q.E.D. for the audience of the Mellon lectures then they should have stayed at home and studied their Aristotle.

But hidden deep beneath the surface of this book there is a thread; it's just that its lovely illustrations, its readings of poems and paintings, its anecdotes about composers, as well as an incongruous extended reading of *The Tempest* have nothing to do with it. It appears erratically and then vanishes for another thirty pages or so. Clear away the pretty distractions and it turns out to be an argument against "the pietistic notion that it is the office of poetry to provide spiritual uplift, ideas to live and die by, elevating maxims, the cloudier the better, and the more disembodied the safer". Poetry should be written and read with a passionate attention to words and the world. It should not be used as an incitement to direct action (Hecht studiously dismisses most political poetry), but rather should be capable of balancing a "contrariety of impulses", the effect of which is "to inhibit any limp tendency to narcissistic solipsism", lending "the poetry itself the rich complexity of actuality".

This attitude leads Hecht to disparage astutely the kind of politicisation of poetry perpetrated by both the likes of Jesse Helms *and* the National Endowment for the Arts, most particularly in the debates of 1992. Politically correct poetry is just as awful as the poetry we can imagine the Republicans reading with satisfaction. This is good sense, but for the rest of the time I can't help wondering why Hecht never engages directly those opinions that contradict his own, or why he doesn't offer readings of the type of poem which he inveighs against and show us, there and then, what's wrong with it. The poet who comes to mind immediately and who was, ironically, nurtured in the same New Critical kindergarten as Hecht, is Adrienne Rich. She has argued this ground already, and Hecht's book would have been many times better if he had taken up this gauntlet. Hecht is one of the best living poets in America, one who is well able to balance many contrarieties of impulses in his poetry, but on the evidence of this book he is incapable of doing so in his prose.

Old Age Travellers

by John Greening

A. R. AMMONS
Tape for the Turn of the Year

Norton, £8.95,
ISBN 0 393 31204 6

Garbage

Norton, £7.50,
ISBN 0 393 31203 8

LINDA PASTAN
Heroes in Disguise

Norton, $8.95,
ISBN 0 393 30922 3

An Early Afterlife

Norton, $10.00,
ISBN 0 393 31381 6

MARGE PIERCY
Eight Chambers of the Heart

Penguin, £7.99,
ISBN 0 14 023637 6

MAY SARTON
Coming into Eighty

Women's Press, £8.99,
ISBN 0 7043 4413 0

JANE COOPER
Green Notebook, Winter Road

Bloodaxe, £7.95,
ISBN 1 85244 311 2

RACHEL HADAS
The Empty Bed

Wesleyan University Press, £8.95,
ISBN 0 8195 1225 7

A. R. AMMONS' *Tape for the Turn of the Year* dates from thirty years ago and Norton have just reissued it alongside his new National Book Award winner, *Garbage*. In case you haven't heard the story, *Tape for the Turn of the Year* began when Archie Ammons decided to put a reel of adding-machine tape into his typewriter. Instantly, he had found a form and at the same time this master of labyrinthine clauses had closure forced on him – albeit 200 pages further

on! He begins, famously, with a bricks-in-the-Tate insouciance –

> today I
> decided to write
> a long
>   thin
>   poem

– and what follows is a wonderful junkshop of a journal from 6th December to 10th January. If you have not read it, or if you only know 'The Really Short Poems', prepare to enjoy yourself.

Since 1965, Ammons' style has put on a little middle-age spread – longer lines, typed on ordinary paper! – but is now even more breathtakingly audacious in its scope. Certainly it is not mere style, not Ashbery:

> this is just a poem with a job to do: and that
>
> is to declare, however roundabout, sideways
> or meanderingly (or in those ways) the perfect
>
> scientific and materialistic notion of the
> spindle of energy:

I can understand how many readers would find Ammons' circumlocutions and digressions infuriating, but they are Byronic essentials, a surprise in every line: "and then one day the weight / whomps down and you jack-spring onto a / different floe or the road you were doing seventy / on rumbles or runs out of road: / meanwhile, baked potatoes are still fine, / split down the middle, buttered up . . ." A. R. Ammons is a profound poet, who knows how to "get the / point reason couldn't, the point delivered below / the level of argument", and *Garbage* is a landfill reeking of rich wisdom, jagged observation, infectious humour and the most salvageable of anecdotes. In essence, it is an elegy upon rejection ("why thrown / out in the first place") and waste. The ruthless philosophising, the unflinching attention to urban squalor may bring C. K. Williams to mind, but Ammons has more fun with his reader and has an eye that goes deeper into creation, into the very nature of creativity.

Linda Pastan

I wish to focus on Linda Pastan's new book, *An Early Afterlife*, but everything applies also to *Heroes in Disguise* (1991). As with A. R. Ammons (as with so much American verse) a great deal hinges on the poet's personality. Linda Pastan's is very likeable. She writes lucid, symmetrical poems, whose ideas never outstay their welcome, whose syntax fits the form like snake into skin. She keeps the side-pressure high on the "long thin" poems, adding just enough spin to keep us on our toes. She returns repeatedly to themes of orderliness (gardening, topiary, that neat line between her parents' beds she longed to vanish down, those squares of polished linoleum that somehow help her contain the emotions associated with a death) and discusses her own will to symmetry in 'Ideal City', an account of an oil painting of a city "of pure perspective" which makes her wish she could "break all the laws of Geometry, / to litter these spotless streets . . ." We feel the poet forcing herself (though less energetically than A. R. Ammons) not to be too conventional: this emerges in the mix of metres and forms as well as in the sweet-sour domestic mood. Nothing obscure here: no clusters of artificially boosted vocabulary, no self-conscious cleverness. Instead, a lot of smokey, dream-haunted lines – "I love the dialects of smoke . . ."; "today I write / of the shadows / flowers make . . ." – with the occasional strand of barbed wire. Loss, change, disappearance – these are her themes. She writes of migratory birds "teaching all of us / with their tail feathers / the true north" and of tree-felling in Eden ("even the complicitous apple"). Death is an ever-present weight, rather than a terror: "For as we turn / the pages of the book / each page grows heavier . . ." and she confronts it vividly in a number of elegies. However, there is perhaps too much trim ease in Linda Pastan's manner at times; her amber and sepia tones begin to feel a little too complacent. "Old men should be explorers", said Eliot. And no doubt meant to include women too.

Marge Piercy's

Selected Poems launch us into a world of character and drama a long way from Linda Pastan's – but then, Piercy is firstly a novelist. Secondly an autobiographer. Alas, the title of "poet" comes a poor third, although in her introduction she claims to be one of the most popular poets in America: "They are the sort of poems people carry in their wallets, put up on their refrigerators or over their computers". Which wasn't quite my own reaction. These pieces are entertaining enough, and maybe even (as

she wants them to be) "useful". She can write compactly, lyrically, powerfully, but she is generally just too aware of her audience, too slack, too eager to impress, shock or please. Where one looks for architecture, one finds rhetoric. Where one looks for propriety, one finds excess. It's simply not the real thing. And, of course, of all these books under review, this is the one you are most likely to find in the shops!

May Sarton

Coming into Eighty is a chronological selection from May Sarton's long poetic career, ranging from work written in the 'thirties to her most recent (hence the title). Born in Belgium, established as an American poet in the school of Edna St. Vincent Millay, the early poems smack more of Yeats:

> ". . . All seems ignoble and I rage
> To have been listed player on this stage".
> At sixty-five that anger conquered fear:
> The old man raged, but he did not despair.
> ('What the Old Man Said')

The recent work in fact shares some of the same flaws as Piercy's, though it is in an utterly different idiom. The rhetoric here is not the streetwise, politically correct, deliberately eye-catching sort: it consists of the flowing robes of the visionary, the wielding of words like "tumultuous", "splendor", "bountiful". But what distinguishes Sarton is her ability to objectify. She also has a broader, if rather old-fashioned, interest in form (see 'In Time Like Air', 1954) although some of her rhymes are very weak. As the book progresses, something leaner, a little more modern emerges. The work from the 'sixties is particularly memorable in its "artful measure / And sweet austerity": 'At Delphi', for instance, or 'Girl with Cello'. I am reminded of Kathleen Raine in the desire for "Poetry, prayer, or call it what you choose / That frees the complicated act of will / And makes the whole world both intense and still". Altogether, May Sarton comes across as wise, warm-hearted, attuned to the spiritual possibilities of the natural world, but lacking that ruthless will to essentials in her actual writing.

Jane Cooper

I was interested to compare May Sarton's thoughts on the nature of creativity ('Journey Towards

Poetry') with those of A. R. Ammons (*Garbage*, Section 6). Jane Cooper, too, explores this area. 'The Green Notebook' of her title is one she imagines "containing all the poems of my life" and elsewhere she writes of trying to write "a poem dense with ordinary detail". Her poetry is in fact suspended on detail of a more surreal kind: dream imagery which colours her deceptively plain narratives of daily life, resulting in something at once familiar yet surprising:

> What is happening to me now that loved faces
> are beginning to float free of their names
> like a tide of balloons, while a dark street
> wide enough only for carriages, in a familiar city,
> loses itself to become South America?
>   ('Childhood in Jacksonville, Florida')

She writes genuine free verse – not so easy as a few thousand Americans seem to believe! – managing to be Whitman and herself in the elegiac 'Long Disconsolate Lines', then to be business-like with the short lines of the next poem, 'Bloodroot'. Varied yet impressively consistent, Jane Cooper has learnt the most important lesson: just how much to leave out. There is a good deal of prose in this collection – a memoir of her father, a vivid and moving piece of autobiography, 'The Children's Ward' – and some work between poetry and prose, that one might call *pensées* (see 'Seventeen Questions about King Kong'). The grand finale is in the mosaicked musical idiom of Epic Modernism: a tribute to Willa Cather. Jane Cooper reminds me of Elizabeth Bishop in her slightly bizarre angle on the world and her painterly attention to colours. But she is also very much a Southerner, who has to ask "Can any white person write this whose ancestors kept slaves?" I feel now that I want to read the *Selected Poems* which Anvil produced in 1984.

Rachel Hadas

wrote the entry for Jane Cooper in the *Oxford Companion*, speaking of her work's "sinewy thought-through quality". The same could be said of her own work. The muscular strengths are appropriately evident in her poem about ballet-dancers "sculpting a carnal maze / of intricate delight". There is much to delight in her new book: lyrical, intelligent, dense, questioning poems, vibrant with symbolic resonance, but always lucid. 'Lunch the Day after Thanksgiving' begins:

> To my right (your left) the steamed-up pane
> doesn't quite hide a line of hungry would-
>
> be lunchers who gaze meaningfully in;
> to my left (your right) low November sun
>
> has just transformed a red and blue plaid elbow
> into a radiant morsel of stained glass
>
> seen out of the corner of my eye
> as happiness always is.

I found these poems spoke to me more than many I read for this review. Hadas's formal enthusiasms are invigorating: quatrain, sonnet, extended Marvellian couplets ('The Friend'), witty Merrillian metaphysics ('The House Beside the Sea'), even some deliberate doggerel. But the book's major theme is what will attract readers – this is a collection haunted by AIDS and Part II centres on elegies for the death of five poets with whom Rachel Hadas worked at Gay Men's Health Crisis, events which were closely followed by the death of her own mother. The formal skills – sometimes carried to almost desperate lengths in the later poems – make for some harrowingly powerful writing. She keeps the incisive satirical note even in elegy:

> That was the spring I squatted on two floors,
> gaping at the bright interiors
> of twin refrigerators left forlorn
> in widely separated parts of town.
> These gleaming dual criteria of lives
> halted halfway through milk or mayonnaise
> (lives not yet ended, moving day by day
> out of the realm where calories hold sway) . . .
>   ('Leftovers')

It is interesting that the best elegies have been by the best formalists (Douglas Dunn, Thom Gunn). Rachel Hadas claims in 'Peculiar Sanctity' "the renaissance of elegy / as the defining genre of our day", proving her case in the force of her own lovingly crafted elegiacs. I think that this and the Ammons are the books I will most return to: the one poet fighting form, resisting closure; the other wooing it, working with it, finally overwhelmed by it. I only hope that Wesleyan U. P.'s distributors make sure *The Empty Bed* fills the shelves.

John Greening's new collections are *The Coastal Path* (Headland) and *The Bocase Stone* (Dedalus).

Rifled Treasury

by Stephen Burt

GJERTRUD SCHNACKENBERG
A Gilded Lapse of Time

Harvill, £7.99,
ISBN 1 86046 018 6

GJERTRUD SCHNACKENBERG USED to be above all a *pleasant* poet, one who combined high-culture learning, difficult forms (rhymed sapphics, villanelles) and reassuring accessibility; the American New Formalist critics of the 1980s accordingly celebrated her work, though some other readers found anthology-pieces like 'Supernatural Love' sugary or slight. Compared to that work, *A Gilded Lapse of Time* – published in America four years ago – is sprawling, unprotected and "difficult", full of lengthy speculations on Italian Renaissance art and artists, the nature of God, the Roman Empire, and the risen Christ. Schnackenberg is sincere, serious, and devoted: the trouble is that the quality of the writing has plummeted. Here is half of section 17 of the 20-section title poem, a hallucinatory pilgrimage-cum-art tour through Ravenna: the poet, leaving Dante's tomb, addresses Dante:

I heard a deeper set of doors slam shut,

A sound reverberating outside the walls of poetry,
As if the doors of the kingdom had closed behind me
With that sound you could not transcribe
After you'd crossed the threshold of the dead
And entered a gate from which you promised
Never to look back, no matter what,

As the doors slammed shut,
And you let your thoughts revolve
Around the bliss of leaving your life behind,
Of clinging in your ascent, and looking up,
Forgetting earth with every step you took –

The "walls of poetry", the doors that "slam shut", the bliss of clinging in an ascent around which thoughts revolve, and the asides like "no matter what" are typical – but it's all typical: this kind of low-pressure, reverent, self-reverent language is the sole building material for most of the book, and

one is exaggeratedly grateful for the intrusion of single demotic words, like "crud". The twentieth and last poem of the Dante sequence begins "Then Gabriel sent down a dream" – of, what else, a dark wood – and continues "I had meant only / To open your book, to study poetry's empty beauty . . ." Profundity, ambition and visionary quality are meant, here, to substitute for line-by-line verbal and aural surprise: readers who believe such a substitution is ever possible in lyric are the ones who will enjoy this book.

Schnackenberg seems to be trying for what medieval rhetoricians called *amplificatio*, drawing out her sentences and periods for as long as she can. At best, her infinitely extensible chains of clauses can suggest obsessions and hypnopompic states, as in 'Soldier Asleep at the Tomb':

You toil through mortar streets
Between the bricks
As if you knew the way,
But really you must admit
You're lost. But really
You must not lose the way.

But later in the same poem comes writing like this:

But when you look out the corner
Of your eye, the heaps of
Flamingo carcasses the soldiers carry
On sagging litters,
As if they had done battle
With the sunset,
become a heap of murdered angels
Pitchforked from a horrifying height.

What *do* murdered angels look like? And how high is horrifying? Elsewhere, there is sheer poeticalness –

Here death is only a flash of world
Unfurled from a rifled
Church treasury, and you are invited
To walk this alluvial wave of gold,

To walk in the labyrinths
Of the angels' howls.

If there were an angels' union it would surely be filing for overtime pay (though Schnackenberg is hardly the first, or tenth, Anglophone poet to use Rilke this way). 'A Monument in Utopia', about Mandelstam (*précis*: Mandelstam was a great poet,

Stalin was evil, I dream of a world in which everything's OK), comprises a wealth of anecdotes mined from memoirs, but also a desktop "blizzard of paper", "multileveled, multipetaled realities", and this: "*They never asked themselves / Whether it was worthwhile / To save the Roman Empire / In order to make it a vast prison / For scores of millions of men*", taken, the copious notes tell us, "from somewhere in Edward Gibbon, *The Decline and Fall of the Roman Empire*". (If Gibbon wrote that, the less Gibbon he.) When the real angel comes for the contemporary poets she will take the shape of a copy-editor, and bring, not peace, but a blue pencil; if she brings scales as well, several of Schnackenberg's graceful, formal earlier poems will belong in one pan, and the lengthy sequences here in the other. Pound and Larkin didn't agree on much, but one said and the other showed that poetry could be "as well-written as prose"; these poems largely aren't, and they left me hoping this genuine poet's next book would resemble her last-but-one.

Stephen Burt writes for the *TLS* and *Thumbscrew*.

C. K. WILLIAMS
GRIEF

Dossie Williams 1914–1995

1.

Gone now, after the days of desperate, unconscious gasping, the reflexive staying alive,
tumorous lungs, tumorous blood, ruined, tumorous liver demanding to live, to go on,
even the innocent bladder, its tenuous, dull golden coin in the slack translucent bag,
gone now, after the months of scanning, medication, nausea, hair loss and weight loss;
remission, partial remission, gratitude, hope, lost hope, anxiety, anger, confusion,
the hours and days of everyday life, something like life but only as dying is like life;
gone the quiet at the end of dying, the mouth caught agape on its last bite at a breath,
bare skull with its babylike growth of new hair thrown back to open the terrified larynx;
the flesh given way but still of the world, lost but still in the world with the living;
my hand on her face, on her brow, the sphere of her skull, her arm, thin, flaccid, wasted;
gone, yet of us and with us, a person, not yet mere dream or imagination, then, gone, wholly,
under the earth, cold earth, cold grasses, cold winter wind, freezing eternity, cold, forever.

2.

Is this grief? Tears took me, then ceased; the wish to die, too, may have fled through me,
but not more than with any moment's despair, the old, surging wish to be freed, finished.
I feel pain, pain for her fear, pain for her having to know she was going, though we must;
pain for the pain of my daughter and son, for my wife whose despair for her mother returned;
pain for all human beings who know they will go and still go as though they knew nothing,
even pain for myself, my incomprehension, my fear of so many stories never begun now
never ending.

But still, is this grief: waking too early, tiring too quickly, distracted, impatient, abrupt,
but still waking, still acting, thinking, working; is this what grief is, is this sorrow enough?
I go to the mirror: someone who might have once felt something merely regards me,
eyes telling nothing, mouth saying nothing, nothing reflected but the things of the world,
nothing told not of any week's, no, already ten days now, any ten days' normal doings.
Shouldn't the face evidence anguish, shouldn't its love and loss and sadness be revealed?
Ineffable, vague, elusive, uncertain, distracted: shouldn't grief have a form of its own,
and shouldn't mind know past its moment of vague, uncertain distraction the sureness of
                                                                                sorrow;
shouldn't soul flinch as we're taught proper souls are supposed to, in reverence and fear?
Shouldn't grief be pure, perfect, complete, reshaping the world in itself, in grief for itself?

3.

Eighty, dying, in bed, tubes in her chest, my mother puts on her morning make up;
the broad, deft strokes of foundation, the blended-in rouge, powder, eye shadow, lipstick;
that concentration with which you must gaze at yourself, that ravenous, unfaltering focus.
Grief for my mother, for whatever she thought her face had to be, to be made every morning;
grief for my mother-in-law in her last declining, destroying dementia, getting it wrong,
the thick ropes of rouge, garish green paint on her lips; mad, misplaced slash of mascara;
grief for all women's faces, applied, created, trying to manifest what the soul seeks to be,
grief for the faces of all human beings, our own faces telling us so much and no more,
offering pain to all who behold them, but which when they turn to themselves, petrify, pose.
Grief for the faces of adults who must gaze in their eyes deeply so as not to glimpse death,
and grief for the young who see only their own relentless and grievous longing for love.
Grief for my own eyes that try to seek truth, even of pain, of grief, but find only approximation.

4.

My face beneath your face, face of grief, countenance of loss, fear, final, irrevocable extinction;
matrix laid upon matrix, mystery on mystery, guise upon guise, semblance, effigy, likeness.
O, to put the face of grief on in the morning; the tinting, smoothing, shining and shaping;
and at the end of the day, to remove it, detach it, emerge from the sorrowful mask.
Stripped now of its raiment, the mouth, caught in its last labored breath finds last resolution,
all the flesh now, stripped of its guises, moves towards its place in the peace of the earth.
Grief for the earth, accepting the grief of the flesh and the grief of our grieving forever;
grief for the flesh and the body and face, for the eyes that can see only into the world,
and the mind that can only think and feel what the world gives it to think and to feel;
grief for the mind gone, the flesh gone, the imperfect pain that must stay for its moment;
and grief for the moment, its partial beauties, attachments, affections, all severed, all torn.

Botanical Haven

by John Redmond

LOUISE GLÜCK
The Wild Iris
Carcanet Press, £8.95,
ISBN 1 85754 223 1

DELIBERATELY OLD-FASHIONED in style and saturated with natural imagery, Louise Glück's sixth collection, *The Wild Iris*, is largely a meditation on her relationship with God. The titles give the flavour. Almost half the poems are either called 'Matins' or 'Vespers', while many of the rest make reference to the seasons: 'End of Summer', 'Retreating Light', 'September Twilight'. In a poem called 'Daisies', one of the book's more self-conscious pieces, she appears to anticipate (but not defuse) criticism of her limited themes.

> Go ahead: say what you're thinking. The garden
> is not the real world. Machines
> are the real world.

But by providing this over-simple opposition, Glück is telling us more about her world than the "real" one. The notable absence of machinery in *The Wild Iris* extends not just to laptops, jump-leads and Chinook helicopters, but even to old technology, to everything produced, and probably everything thought, by Gutenberg, Edison and the Wright brothers. The few man-made instruments which do appear – a garden trowel, a metal spoon (the metal being unusual enough to mention) – seem so naturalised that they're already growing roots and when one poem mentions a mailbox, one feels it belongs to a world without the U. S. Postal Service – without postal services, even. With its maples and birches, its lilies and blueberries, its wave on wave of buttercups roses, foxgloves, and violets, it is a landscape from which the modern world has been carefully pruned away. What remains is a serene little oasis, rather like an English Garden Centre or Tom Bombadil's enchanted forest in *The Lord of the Rings*, where it would be less surprising to see one of the High Elves than someone sporting an *Oasis* T-shirt.

Inside this botanical haven a string of unashamedly simple metaphors flourish: God as a sunset; renewal as a fountain; a human being as a falling leaf.

Light and Darkness engage, as they always seem to, in a perpetually abstract and inconclusive struggle, while the poet's Heart (sometimes her Soul) potters from one defining emotional moment to another, from "stillness", "silence" and "joy" to "fear", "rage" and "despair". Only John and Noah, the poet's husband and son (with their appropriately Biblical names) appear from time to time to remind us of the Human Race. When God weighs in with a few words, he sounds remarkably like Glück, a well-meaning old aunt determined to improve us:

> As I get further away from you
> I see you more clearly.
> Your souls should have been immense by now,
> not what they are,
> small talking things –

Combining intimacy with indeterminacy, "you" is a favourite word in contemporary poetry and here almost every poem contains the second person pronoun, giving the impression of an unbroken dialogue. We can see this when the exasperation which God so understandably feels with "small talking things" is reciprocated, and Glück complains about His silence:

> Forgive me if I say I love you: the powerful
> are always lied to since the weak are always
> driven by panic. I cannot love
> what I can't conceive, and you disclose
> virtually nothing . . .

Characteristically, Glück's presentation of this very old theme wobbles: The powerful are *always* lied to? The weak are *always* driven by panic? The language, too, is uncertain. One is more likely to say "you disclose / virtually nothing" to a recalcitrant tax consultant than to the Almighty. In other poems, Glück bravely uses archaic diction ("giveth", for example) but here she is unsure whether to be formal or colloquial, as the change from "cannot" to "can't" indicates.

Thinking of poetic composition, Marianne Moore reminds us that "omissions are not accidents". Is it not strange, then, that what is wrong with *The Wild Iris* is not that it omits the modern world (that is only a symptom) but that it omits the accidental? The poems are too predictable and controlled, belonging to a world where all contingencies have been excluded. Like the prayers in old-time catechisms, their homely simplicity mainly serves to provide comfort, not communication. Away and read *Flowers and Insects*!

MARILYN HACKER
DIRECTIONS

You knew the right title for all these years.
Now the book's in your hands. The book has changed
key, cadence, resonated and resolved strange
dissonances. Days, stanzas disappear,
emerge again, seen otherwise. Yes, we're
hovering over it, translucent, stained
glass saints through whom light filters down, a rain
of colors on an upturned face, in tears
or, merely, questioning. Or, we're the river
whose motion you can follow through the trees
you look out at on a grey day. A sliver
of light crosses the notebook on your knees
where words dappling the water rearrange
themselves. Outside's the road that brought you here.

Outside yourself, the road that brought you where
you live now disappears into those trees,
which disappear themselves, the century's
avatars, in fog. The thickening air
makes you think, because you're who you are,
of other woods, in Ukraine, Germany,
Poland, where fog, like anonymity,
hung on bland branches during the massacre.
A continent of disconnected lights
extends in front of you, and then its stark
contours recede. You look at your own hand
– which wields tools, strokes strings, touches a lover, writes –
and close your book because it's getting dark.
How can you sing their songs in a strange land?

How can I sing their songs in a strange land?
Which river is the river in the song?
Which town was Zion, which was Babylon?
Which language do I still misunderstand
in patches? The FN's in Marignane's
mairie, also in Orange, in Toulon,
while rumors of exclusion are pronounced
daily in flatland mid-American.
The city street's slicked down in the late rain.

Its dim-lit, curtained windows, big as doors,
half-close on half-written biographies
of polyglot and stateless ancestors
whose surnames were folk-tale geography:
rose-garden, golden mountain, silver stone.

Goldenberger, Weingarten, Szylberstyn,
had wholesale menswear Showrooms on this street
– *maison fondée en mil-neuf-cent-vingt-huit* –
cut and sewed suits in cramped workrooms behind
the shopfronts, or upstairs: noisy, benign
family fiefs. There was one year they cut
and sewed yellow cloth stars. Then the shops shut.
A few returned, repainted their old signs.
Elsewhere, my mother's tailor father Max
Rosengarten's hired workers straggled up
six flights: finishers, pressers, a bookkeeper
– like my father's mother Gisela
Wilde. Now I live above the shop.
A piecework landscape frays behind their backs.

A pieced landscape displayed behind the backs
of saints in blue and scarlet jewel-hues
bathes meditative unconverted Jews
with light that pools, prismatic, in the lakes
round votive candles melted down to wax
they lit before they slipped into the pews.
Another generation paid their dues.
The Mass is something like illicit sex.
(They'd have to sit upstairs behind a grille
if their cathedral were the orthodox
synagogue, whose women embroidered this
minute brocaded armchair for a *briss*
they watched from purdah.) On a green glass hill,
some errant ewes survey the docile flocks.

You've errands. You survey the docile flocks
trooping down into the subway in the heat.
(You're glad you work on Twenty-Second Street,
a healthy amble of eleven blocks.)
A hundred books are shrink-wrapped in a box –
like bricks of juice. Bank; druggists . . . Will you treat
yourself to those new boots? To celebrate

what? It seems pointless, that's the paradox:
a suite of choices as gratuitous
as a coin flipped into a blue chalk
hopscotch grid drawn on cement, which spun
down "lover", "mother", enigmatic "us".
But I'm imagining your morning walk
from the long distance of my afternoon.

From the long distance of my afternoon,
a smell of frites comes up from the cafés.
A scruffy jazz group (four French white boys) plays
ragtime beneath the traffic light: trombone,
French horn, sax, banjo. You're as good as gone,
you wrote, and went. We're still alive. The day's
muddle of heat condenses in a haze
of car exhaust.
                    In whatever time-zone
we reach each other cautiously, we touch
in tentatives of words, we frame our fears
with Ashkenazi irony. I keep
that distance – it's the place from which I watched
you, younger, going somewhere in your sleep.
You knew the right direction all these years.

MIKE SHARPE
COCKROACHES

The very word clicks like stiff wings,
Pulsing the walls.
The peg-rug seems wet
With the gleam of their bodies,
Rocking the throat with the crunch
Underfoot.

This was the scuttling evil
They watched, just married,
Holding hands in the candle light
Of their first rented room.

Always, afterwards, every darkness threatened,
Every surface whispered
With a sudden unsheathing of wings.

An Angled Plough

by Ian Sansom

IAIN CRICHTON SMITH
Collected Poems
Carcanet, £9.99,
ISBN 1 85754 245 2

IAIN CRICHTON SMITH was born in Glasgow in 1928 and brought up in Bayble, on the isle of Lewis. He spoke only Gaelic till he was 5, and then had to go to school and learn English, an experience which he describes as a "blow to the psyche, an insult to the brain", a "classic recipe for schizophrenia" (fortunately, only his temporal coding seems to have been affected: his early work is in English; only later did he go back to Gaelic). At seventeen he left Lewis to go to university in Aberdeen, and subsequently taught in the west of Scotland. He has described himself as a "double man riddled with guilt", displaced and exiled from language. Yet what strikes one reading his *Collected Poems* is the sheer equanimity of his temper and the humility of his disposition. Not all Scots poets are like MacDiarmid.

His work is simple, which is not to say dim, or easy. There is a quiet lack of fuss about it: no knick-knacks, no miscellanea. The language is plain and unadorned: it is poetry without spin, without pleats or vibrato or wobble (in fact the nearest he comes to archness or irony is in his translations from his own Gaelic – in his 1975 collection *The Permanent Island* – which suggests that the mother-tongue is somehow naturally more playful, more lively). What he calls the "*ceol na mara*", the music of the sea and the "Free Church air" blow throughout: pure, raw, self-sufficient and self-effacing, with no sign of a confessional, nor a whiff of pomp or incense. But the simplicity is hard won. "To be pure is not difficult", he writes in 'The Glass of Water', "it's impossible", and even to be good takes ages: his later work is much to be preferred to his early stuff, which is cluttered with bits from Yeats and Auden. *The Long River* (1955), *The White Noon* (1959), and *Thistles and Roses* (1961) are OK: *A Life* (1986) and *The Village* (1989) are outstanding.

Growing up in the Free Church tradition on Lewis left him, he says, "unhealthily concerned with religion, so that I find I do not wholly believe in poems of the moment but rather in poems morally shaped". His own moral shapes are well-defined and rounded, with his poetry often acting like a pivot – as in 'Studies in Power', where "straining forces" are "harmonised sincerely" – or as a meeting place for what he calls in 'The White Air of March' the "vertical horizontal". It is all a matter of balance, as the young Malcolm realises in Smith's novel *The Last Summer* (1969), a semi-autobiographical depiction of adolescent life on Lewis in the 1940s: "Shifting a bit, Malcolm looked sideways and noticed for the first time that the bible was lying on top of a Penguin *New Writing*".

Smith's attitude towards religion is actually rather frosty and agnostic, but his work is open towards higher things, with more than occasional rumours of glory: there is much lightning, dazzling, glittering, and shining, for example. 'In Luss Churchyard' is typically highly-charged:

Here however a skull, there crossed bones
leap out with tigerish instancy, like fire
burning through paper: with a savage force
punch through electric noon where the hands perspire
and prickle with the sun.

Yet all the light in the poems brings little warmth: light, for Smith, more often means judgement – as in 'The Widow', where "the bare electric light / mocked my new body" – and he is himself given to bursts of fury, or at least to bouts of righteous anger. A teacher for thirty years, he seems to despair over mass education. The famous early poem 'A Young Highland Girl Studying Poetry' is a fine example of writing against itself:

Poetry drives its lines into her forehead
like an angled plough across a bare field.
I've seen her kind before, of the live and the dead
who bore humped creels when the beating winds
were wild.
Nor did they know much poetry but were skilful
at healing children, bringing lambs to birth.
. . .

And she – like them – should grow along these valleys
bearing bright children, being kind to love.
Simple affection needs no complex solace
nor quieter minds abstractions of the grave.

Those few occasions on which Smith fails to maintain his composure, the moments when he loses his balance, are when he gives in to speculating about his own method as a poet, a method which amounts to a kind of tweedy Highland Imagism: "There is no metaphor", he portentously pronounces in 'Deer on the High Hills', "The stone is stony . . . The rain is rainy and the sun is sunny. The flower is flowery and the sea is salty".

Phenomenology doth not a poem make.

But such slips are the exception rather than the rule. Throughout a life's work he has managed to remain scrupulous without becoming a scrupuland and serious without becoming conceited: there is no guile in him. "The Highlander", he writes in an essay 'Real People in a Real Place', "has a concept of *cliù*, which roughly means 'reputation', and such a concept implies that a man who has it may be considered useful to the community, not glorified, but respected". Smith is useful. He deserves our respect.

Ian Sansom writes for the the *Guardian*, the *TLS*, and the *LRB*.

At the Turnpike in Space

by Harry Clifton

CHARLES BOYLE
Paleface
Faber, £6.99,
ISBN 0 571 17729 8

SINCE THE LATER Romantics, poets have been fighting a kind of two-hundred-years' war with the word Pale. The brief has been to get rid of it in the interests of health over sickliness, iron specificity over waffle. Charles Boyle reinstates it in the title of his book, only to knock it to pieces with the thirty-four-gun salvo of the poems themselves. Whatever else one says about this collection, it should be a landmark in the history of a word. Where once there was Romantic pale, now there is National health pale. Instead of palely loitering, our paleface stares through suburban windows, doctors cert in hand, glad of a reprieve from the hated desk-job.

> . . . strangers walk by
> maybe five minutes sooner or later, no more,
> than their usual time
>
> from the bus, coming home: as if this were some
> daily police
> reconstruction, as if a witness's memory
> might be jogged into total recall.
>
> ('Overtime')

Not that the palefaces aren't also a tribe of sorts. In an extended sequence entitled 'Velcro', their habits, desires and artefacts, be they hardcore videos, ejector seats or whatever, are interleaved to ironic effect with those of some imagined tribe in the Syrian desert. It isn't a new device, as the Faber back catalogue, with poets discovering Lokis, Crees and dead Mistah Kurtzes in their own back gardens, will testify. Here, it is by turns funny, depressing, and as a black joke upon "civilisation" a bit long-drawn-out perhaps. But it serves to condense the bourgeois self-hatreds, blockages and blind lashings out at fate that characterise the rest of the book. For we are among those of "a certain age", for whom sex and religion, the old sustaining forces of life and the spirit, are a hollow Larkinesque joke.

> Sex: *see under* alabaster;
> Earhart, Amelia; Friday.
> *see also* tongs.
>
> It's not that they don't
> enjoy it, but are often inhibited
> by their distracting need
>
> to rationalize the gap
> between the gritty norm
> and their culture's pellucid ideal.

The Larkin of 'Going, going', the voice from the bricked-in boiling that is Britain, is the presiding ghost. Not only for the terminal vision, but more especially for the conscious embrace of limitation –

> . . . I'm a man,
> I've been around if not far, I can hum a few tunes,

my patience is finite, I swing my arms as I walk.

('A Certain Age')

– and for the use of a quotidian language, gritty with impurities that seem breathed in and out without apparent damage;

My life accused me: paleface, it said, I deserve better.
Is this or is this not an advanced post-industrial

democracy?

Useless explaining the menopause, or that one child

in three
is born below the poverty line.

('Monday')

If there is a difference, it is that Larkin, for all his pessimism, still retains and expresses a sense of the reality of places, while Boyle, though he mentions Leytonstone and Lyme Regis, makes them sound like refuelling stations in outer space. Here and there are one and the same, as in 'Switzerland', where a colleague once known who gets a fancy job can at least have revenge wreaked upon him by turning him into a character in a virtual reality scenario. Nor could one guess from 'In the Middle Atlas' whether Boyle had actually been there or simply imagined it, though the *denouement* is predictably apocalyptic:

I climbed the hundred and ninety-nine steps
of the ruined minaret without pausing for breath.
Cars made way, women took their children in hand
so I could land without causing undue damage.

If places are interchangeable, so are times, as in 'Fast Forward', 'Later the Same Era' and 'Dutch, 17th century'. But the atmosphere stays the same, one of clenched-teeth domesticity, nostalgia for not-terribly-misspent youth and political impotence. Marriage, children and work are the determinants. How welcome they are it is hard to say, for little that is directly personal gets through the mesh of *de rigueur* cynicism, unless one excepts the affectionate lines that make up 'Figurine' or the lovers' whispered "forever" behind McMaster's barn in 'New Mains 1864'. By now there is something almost touchingly English about emotional dissociation, but it does make for incompleteness in an otherwise highly accomplished collection – as if some negative reflex in the poet keeps killing off

any would-be celebrant that might get a word in. Dying falls are worked towards and artfully achieved time and again, but the range of emotion stays narrow. Is it fear of feeling or absence of feeling that produces the schoolboy caricature of religion in 'The Optometrist'?

Let's pick a desert,
you and I,
filter it somehow,
fire it to the degree you say,
grind it etcetera
and see what we can see –
angel number 101
break-dancing on your tiepin?

Either way, it seems a variation on Larkin's Irish sixpence in the collection box in 'Church Going'. Also Larkin-influenced, this time by 'Faith Healing', is the much better 'Miracle at Shepherd's Bush' which covers the same ground more humanly and compassionately, though still avoiding choice at the end. But God or the absence of God seem hardly at issue in a middle-age suspended, as this one is, between "The things I did to Susie" ('Serial') way back when, and a Life to Come comprising personal effects auctioned off in a car-boot sale ('White City'). Death in a way is less important than Unfulfilment, the one Negative whittled away at relentlessly, often brilliantly, at times to the point of affectation. The final lines of 'Sheds', which are also the final lines of the book, bring the two together with a rare directness of feeling.

Exhaustion, waste, relief
at being one again with nature –
and still a kind of reckless belief
that just one more day, another hour of light
would have seen it through.

Charles Boyle isn't the first and won't be the last poet to conflate his own middle-age with the collapse of civilisation in general. It's an old statement, and it needs to be remade periodically with the kind of modulated bitterness so expertly expressed in this collection. But there are other pastures too, not all of them in cyberspace.

Harry Clifton's latest collection, *Night Train through the Brenner* (Gallery), was reviewed by Michael Hulse in the last issue.

THE SONNET HISTORY

JOHN WHITWORTH
THE ROARING FORTIES

Who won the War? The bloody Yanks, but never
Poor bloody us, no strut, no style, no cash,
Just power-cuts, ration-books and queues for ever.
But Art is free and Art should make a splash.

We want extravagance and ormolu,
Black market nylons, marzipan and waste.
Great God! We've had enough of making do,
High mindedness and horrible good taste.

We've had enough of the austerely English.
We want the vatic chant, the Celtic mist,
Poems that leave you out-of-breath and tinglish,
Poems that leave you feeling slightly pissed.

The *Zeitgeist* labours with ecstatic cries,
And Dylan Thomas squalls between her thighs.

Amor Diving

by Alison Combes

ANNEMARIE AUSTIN
The Flaying of Marsyas
Bloodaxe, £6.95,
ISBN 1 85224 328 7

JOHN GLENDAY
Undark
Peterloo, £6.95,
ISBN 1 871471 60 5

PAUL GROVES
Menage à Trois
Seren, £5.95,
ISBN 1 85411 147 7

MARION LOMAX
Raiding the Borders
Bloodaxe, £6.95,
ISBN 1 85224 352 X

IT'S INTERESTING HOW when reviewing more than one book at a time the human brain seems to strive to connect them but certainly common features did emerge from the books under consideration. All the texts selected are second or third collections. Two of the poets are Scottish; three might be described as Celts. All demonstrate the usual concern about matters of death, heredity and regeneration. But more subtle concerns about the construction of memory and the difference between truth and fact are also articulated by each of them.

Annemarie Austin

Austin concerns herself with the difference between perceived truth and established fact in her third collection, *The Flaying of Marsyas*. Indeed her central thesis would appear to be that fact is easily delineated whilst truths are less easily articulated and rarely if ever understood by anyone else. Truth, she seems to suggest in her opening poem, is the business of the gods. All apparently know this; the wise accept it; an artist – and more particularly a poet – will be driven to challenge it as Marsyas did: "the satyr who did what the poet has to do / and challenged heaven with his flight of song". From

this first poem and from its companion 'Marsyas in Hell', we gather that the satyr (and implicitly the poet) always knew an attempt to communicate the truth would be doomed because his version of truth could only ever be partial, inferior to that of a god by definition:"That was a Faustian Compact and he knew what he was about – / impossible to beat a god, unthinkable to surpass / such superhuman skill, yet he was bound to try".

According to Austin, the poet's tragedy and triumph are both located in the last line – that s/he is bound to try to surpass the easily delineated and communicate her version of a deeper, emotional truth. Yet sometimes it is possible to try too hard and Austin can be too didactic. For although the early poems in the sequence work well, that which introduces the second section of the text, 'The Sensible Child Meets Marsyas in the Wood', strives to describe the response of a dispassionate observer to the scene that inspired this sequence, and provokes no greater emotional or intellectual response than a superficial reading of the fairy story to which it explicitly refers. If she wishes to instruct her audience in the visible horror of the Satyr/poet's death, then the lesson would have been easier for us to learn from the gruesome snuff poem which opens the third section of the book. As 'Goat Song' states: "This is tragedy in the purest terms: / the perpendicular dive down / from the branches spread like arms / to the blood-puddled ground, / / and the god turned artisan / at work with the flensing knife, / unpicking pelt and skin / beneath the sacrificial tree".

Perhaps this collection should be read as the work of an artist practising new melodies on new pan pipes. We wait to hear what the final version sounds like. In the meantime, we have no intention of flaying the poet alive.

John Glenday

The relationship between truth and fact is also a preoccupation of John Glenday in his second collection, *Undark*. In 'Annunciation', the narrator and his female opponent debate the species classification of an angel and the nature of its wings. The facts of the matter cannot be ascertained: has anyone ever been able to dissect and therefore classify an angel? Even in 'Undark', the title poem, there is conflict between the perceived beauty of the radium-based paint used on watch dials and the carcinogenic properties inherent in that radioactive substance. Throughout these poems all that is beautiful is at least frail: "Beautiful it is, and damned / not to last, only endure".

Unlike Austin, Glenday seems unsure of his perceptions and fearful of the world just beyond his perceptions where death always waits to seize the unsuspecting: the father drowned in 'Famous Last Words', the murder victim in 'Penny's Dream', the radiant ghosts in 'Undark'. His semantic uncertainty is reflected in Glenday's style too: his syntax can be as precise as a political manifesto ('The Snow Queen') or as convoluted as the spiral of a nautilus shell ('Preserve Me, Mortal'). Only when he is sure of his ground – when he recounts personal memories or when the facts of a situation are well established, as in 'Undark' and 'Pale Flower' – does he utilise the syntax of everyday speech. It is at these times that Glenday speaks most clearly to us – when, to use Austin's metaphor again, instead of worrying about the intricacy of his finger work on those panpipes, he lets the simplicity of his melodies move us by themselves.

Paul Groves

Linguistic simplicity seems to be something which Paul Groves mastered long ago. For the language of his second collection, *Menage à Trois*, is measured, always controlled, whether he chooses rhymed or free verse. This could account for the success of the work in his current collection – all of which has, according to his press release, already been published elsewhere. Facts too are something which he handles deftly as in the very first poem of this new book he remembers the recent death of a friend and states that the tragedy of this event lies not in abstract, philosophical truths but in the experience of mundane facts: "Your children miss the lifting of the latch, your presence in the hall. / A cup of tea. A piece of cake. Your chair. / Your television. Here's the pen you used. / Your toothbrush stays upstairs. Your underwear / is in a drawer".

And Groves holds to this article of faith throughout the rest of the collection. New York is vicariously experienced via a murder tour and green tea ice cream whilst the stresses of competing with the neighbours in suburbia are reduced to the regular analysis of next door's designer-filled rubbish sacks. Groves certainly has an eye for detail. In fact, in poems like 'Solomon Islands Idyll', this attention can appear disquieting, even distasteful. For these poems which strive to anatomise male desire

can often seem little more than boys' playground jokes. Yet when Groves forgets to be clever, forgets to write laddish poems about the nature of male desire and gets on with writing the rhyming poems which he seems to find most natural, then the content of his work sometimes transcends the constraints of his chosen form. When he writes about marital strife and BSE as discussed at dinner parties in the home counties or when he describes the drunken aftermath of some middle-class wedding, then his work speaks most clearly. If I could say only one thing to Groves in the masterclass, it would probably be: slow down and trust your audience to discern the sentiment behind your music for themselves.

Marion Lomax

Trusting the audience seems to be a concept that Marion Lomax has very little difficulty with in her second collection from Bloodaxe, *Raiding the Borders*. For although Lomax clearly deals with the same subjects as her predecessors: the death of loved ones – here her mother – the importance of family and the comfort of memory, her understanding of these situations appears clear and is coherently communicated, usually in Standard English and using the syntax of everyday speech. All of these factors facilitate access and make her work extremely beguiling, but it is probably the construction of the second section, 'Amor Diving', which makes this collection so compelling. For in the poems which return to the subject of her mother's death, Lomax revisits the established facts of the case incessantly, yet each time she does so she presents a different context for her grief, so we understand not just what happened to whom, where and when but also how the person remembering the facts remakes memories to suit her current situation.

This is a focused and stylish collection by a writer confident in the universal appeal of her message, secure in the facts of her work, which are personal, and in her ability to communicate about a subject that matters to her: coming to terms with loss. This was my favourite of the four collections because it seemed to have been written by the poet most at ease with herself and least self-conscious about her art. Ultimately, for me she was the writer who confronted issues about death and family most successfully and who recognised the consolations that memory can present to us all.

Angry Summers

by Tony Curtis

IDRIS DAVIES

The Complete Poems of Idris Davies

Ed. Dafydd Johnston,
University of Wales Press, £39.95,
ISBN 0 7083 1272 1

THE WORK OF Idris Davies is known by few readers of poetry in England, but he has a claim to be recognised as one of the outstanding working class poets of the century. Published in the mid-century by Dent and Faber & Faber, Davies was championed by T. S. Eliot who said of his poems, "They are the best poetic document I know about a particular epoch in a particular place, and I think that they really have a claim to permanence".

In Wales, Idris Davies has been in print almost continuously over the last twenty-five years and his influence on my generation of poets and poetry readers has been as important as that of the two Thomases, Dylan and Ronald Stuart. Dylan Thomas seemed too loud and difficult, falling out of favour as the taste for neo-Romanticism and grand metaphor passed; R. S. Thomas certainly led by example in his protests for nationalism and against the polluting influence of English and American aggressive capitalism. But as our pits died on their feet and were pushed into mass graves by that vindictive woman, Thatcher, a sense of national identity was more easily assimilated by absorbing the heritage in Davies's *Gwalia Deserta* and *The Angry Summer*, than by trying to emulate the spare, cerebral poems of R. S. Thomas as he wrestled with an elusive God in distant Lleyn.

The Complete Poems of Idris Davies is an important work of publishing and scholarship. Dafydd Johnston, who has recently been made Professor of Welsh at University College, Swansea, has placed those two collections at the head of this book and argues for their importance. There are fifty poems from Davies's collections, but of course *Gwalia Deserta* has thirty-six poems or sections and *The Angry Summer* fifty. In addition there are one hundred and seventy-three poems from periodicals and one hundred and twenty-three unpublished poems. The annotations are generous and draw pertinently from Davies's correspondence and his unpublished fiction.

Both major poems should be read in their entirety for the insight they give into a failing industrial society in the period between the wars. Poem XV from *Gwalia Deserta* will be known to many as a folk hit from the Sixties:

Oh what can you give me?
Say the sad bells of Rhymney.

Is there hope for the future?
Cry the brown bells of Merthyr.

It is that ability to sing out in protest and then draw the reader into the despair of the Depression years with the grit of a documentary film-maker that makes Idris Davies such a powerful voice. Here is Poem XII.

There's a concert in the village to buy us boots and
bread,
There's a service in the chapel to make us meek and
mild,
And in the valley town the draper's shop is shut.
The brown dogs snap at the stranger in silk,
And the winter ponies nose the buckets in the street.
The "Miners' Arms" is quiet, the barman half afraid,
And the heroes of newspaper columns on explosion day
Are nearly tired of being proud.
But the widow on the hillside remembers a bitterer day,
The rap at the door and the corpse and the crowd,
And the parson's powerless words.
Her daughters are in London serving dinner to my
lord,
And her single son, so quiet, broods on his luck in the
queue.

It is a fine piece of controlled anger; passionate and at the same time self-aware, conscious of the mediation of suffering by a distant English press, a patronising English upper class.

Davies was moved to tears and rage when he witnessed the unemployed marching through the streets of London. It was a fate he was closer to than any other poet of those years. He had gone down the pit as a boy, had lost a finger in an accident, but then had directed his time to reading and study and had qualified in Leicester as a teacher and taught in London and lastly in Wales through the 'thirties and 'forties, until his death at 48 in 1953.

He enjoyed the support of the London Welsh literary scene focused on Foyle's and Griff's Bookshop and never lost his command of the Welsh language. Like many an ex-pat, Idris Davies was inclined to idealise the community values of his Wales; his work was also inspired by Keats, Shelley, Wordsworth and Yeats, powerful voices he had to work through in order to hear his own; voices sometimes too loud for his own to be heard. But although he never achieved the majesty of Dylan Thomas, Idris Davies had a deeper involvement with the realities of life in south Wales and out of his commitment to the memories of his youth and the angry ideals of his ambitions for his people, he produced a body of work which this impressive collection presents for a wider audience.

> Mrs Evans fach, you want butter again.
> How will you pay for it now, little woman
> With your husband out on strike, and full
> Of the fiery language? Ay, I know him,
> His head is full of fire and brimstone
> And a lot of palaver about communism,
> And me little Dan the Grocer
> Depending so much on private enterprise.
> What, depending on the miners and their
> Money too? O yes, in a way, Mrs Evans,
> Yes, in a way I do, mind you.
> Come tomorrow, little woman, and I'll tell you then
> What I have decided overnight.
> Go home now and tell that rash red husband of yours
> That your grocer cannot afford to go on strike
> Or what would happen to the butter from
>   Carmarthen?
> Good day for now, Mrs Evans fach.

This is only superficially in the same vein as *Under Milk Wood*. The accuracy of voice and the conflicting exercise of power and dependency which this scene represents pulls the reader into an engagement with the issues of community and capitalism; that is still relevant in the valleys of the sole remaining mine, the Tower Colliery success story of buy-out and syndicalism.

You have, no doubt, read Auden and MacNeice and Spender and Orwell; now turn to Davies. His best work, *The Angry Summer: a poem of 1926*, with its shifting voices and personae is a collage of political verse, lyricism and dramatic monologue which is more engaged than exercises in Mass Observation and more acute than the arm's length sympathies of his privileged English contemporaries.

SOME CONTRIBUTORS

Iain Bamforth's *Open Workings* is forthcoming from Carcanet.

Paul Bailey's new novel *Kitty and Virgil* will be published by Fourth Estate later this year.

BIFF's new collection of *Guardian* cartoons 1991–'96 *The Missing Years* will be published by Icon Books in the Autumn.

Wayne Burrows is currently preparing a first collection.

Ian Caws' collection *Herrick's Women* is due from the University of Salzburg Press this summer.

Tony Curtis's latest collection is *War Voices* (Seren, 1995).

Donald Davie's posthumous collection *Poems and Melodramas* will be published by Carcanet in the Autumn.

Christine Despardes is an American poet; 'The Parachute' is her first published poem.

Michael Donaghy's latest collection is *Errata* (Oxford Poets, 1993).

Helen Dunmore's novel *A Spell of Winter* (Viking) won the £30,000 Orange Prize.

Alistair Elliot's *My Country* is published by Carcanet.

Fiachra Gibbons is an Editor of *The Printer's Devil*.

Marilyn Hacker's latest collection is *Winter Numbers* (Norton).

Michael Henry's latest collection is *Panto Sphinx* (Enitharmon).

Tobias Hill's collection *City of Clocks* is forthcoming from Oxford Poets.

Gwyneth Lewis's first collection *Parables and Faxes* won the Aldeburgh Poetry Prize and was shortlisted for the Forward.

Tim Liardet's second collection *Fellini Beach* was published by Seren in 1994.

Edna Longley's *The Living Steam: literature and revisionism in Ireland* was published by Bloodaxe in 1994.

Gerald Mangan's collection *Waiting for the Storm* was published by Bloodaxe in 1990.

Maureen Mcnaughtan was awarded a Scottish Arts Council bursary in 1986.

Arvind Krishna Mehrotra is a leading Indian poet and editor of *The Oxford Anthology of Twelve Modern Indian Poets*.

Paul Muldoon's *New Selected Poems 1968–1994* will be reviewed in the next issue.

Cate Parish is an American poet resident in this country.

Clare Pollard is 17 – this is her first published poem.

Neil Powell's *Roy Fuller: Writer and Society* was published by Carcanet in 1995.

Justin Quinn's first collection *The 'O'o'a'a Bird* (Carcanet) was shortlisted for the Forward Prize.

John Redmond writes for *Thumbscrew* and the *TLS*.

Deryn Rees-Jones' book of essays *Consorting with Angels: Modern Women Poets* will be published by Bloodaxe in 1997.

Neil Rollinson's first collection *A Spillage of Mercury* was published by Cape in June.

Carole Satyamurti's latest collection is *Striking Distance* (Oxford Poets, 1995).

Mike Sharpe has published in *Poetry Wales* and the *Spectator*.

Peter Snowdon lives in Paris.

Margaret Speak's first collection *The Firefly Cage* will be published by Redbeck Press in 1997.

Matthew Sweeney's anthology *Emergency Kit*, co-edited with Jo Shapcott, will be published by Faber in the Autumn.

John Whitworth's *The Sonnet History of Modern Poetry*, illustrated by Gerald Mangan, will be published by Peterloo in 1997.

C. K. Williams' *New & Selected Poems* (Bloodaxe) was reviewed by Jane Duran in *PR* Vol 85 No 4, 1995.

NEWS/COMMENT

NORTH AND SOUTH

Reading between the lines of the little magazines, a tit-for tat war seems to have broken out between the Huddersfield Heavies (see James Keery's identification of its leading hoods in Vol 86 No 1, p88) and the equally terrifying Thumbscrew Tormenters based in Oxford. In *Thumbscrew* No 3, 1995, Ian Sansom attempted to demolish Simon Armitage's rather generally accepted high standing ("a compendium of all that is pseudo, mal-dicted and calloused in the underworld of the English language" – a crib from Myles na gCopaleen, if you wondered). Now Tim Cumming has riposted in *Sunk Island Review* that Glyn Maxwell is nbg either.

Hardy once said that a book of poems could be made to yield any interpretation as to merit you like depending on the preconceived ideas of the reader. These pieces suggest that poetry is lining up along tribal/regional lines, and that prejudice is taking the place of literary criticism. As far as Maxwell and Armitage go, the *Review* values them pretty well equally. Temperamentally, most people will be inclined to prefer one to the other, but they are two gifted poets who, incidentally, value each other's work very highly. We are fortunate to have both of them writing together. As for the geographical squabbles: this is a very small country. The *Review's* role in all this is clear: it is to try to live up to Edna Longley's words: "As a refuge from local commissars . . . [to give] English language poetry some freedom of circulation".

Having lauded the arrival of *Thumbscrew* it is only fair to add that the issue of *Sunk Island Review* in question, 'Spleen', is required reading and the best magazine we've seen since . . . you've guessed. It has Jonathan Coe on the poetry of B. S. Johnson, Sean O'Brien's intro to his forthcoming Bloodaxe critical book, Jonathan Davidson with a timely attack on drivelling blurbs (eg "We see the energies of narrative and image combining to produce a poetry of complexity, yet with greater ease and direction than some of his previous books"), and poems by Ken Smith, Brendan Cleary, Graham Mort and others (every single contributor is male, one has to note).
Spleen: Sunk Island New Writing is available from Sunk Island Publishing, PO Box 74, Lincoln LN1 1QG. price £5 plus p&p.

CONDUCTOR OF CHAOS

Evidence for the Shared Nonsense Theory of the Avant Garde (see 'How the Century Lost its Poetry', Vol 86 No 1, p3) comes straight from the horse's mouth in Iain Sinclair's introduction to *Conductors of Chaos* (Picador), a major new alternative anthology, which will be reviewed in the next issue:

> The work I value is that which seems most remote, alienated, fractured. I don't claim to "understand" it but I like having it around. The darker it grows outside the window, the worse the noises from the island, the more closely do I attend to the mass of instant-printed pamphlets that pile up around my desk. The very titles are pure adrenalin: *Satyrs and Mephitic Angels, Tense Fodder, Hellhound Memos, Civic Crime, Alien Skies, Harpmesh Intermezzi, A Pocket History of the Soul*. You don't need to read them, just handle them: feel the sticky heat creep up through your fingers.

THINGS YOU DIDN'T KNOW ABOUT NEWGEN

> A more recent (and sinister) phenomenon, the "New Generation" poets, have arrived in our midst like pod people. They are eternally not-quite-young and they feed on images of blight. It's a definite bonus if they come from Scotland (better subsidies and a chance to write off some of the BBC's compulsory regional coverage). They were invented by marketing men, hyped into existence with seemingly fictitious occupations and previous histories dreamt up by Poetry Society copywriters.
> (Iain Sinclair, introduction to *Conductors of Chaos*)

POETS WIN PRIZES

Jorie Graham has won the Pulitzer Prize for *The Dream of the Unified Field: Selected Poems 1974-1994*, published in the UK by Carcanet. Graham's poetry has attracted a range of admirers including John Ashbery, Helen Vendler and Michael Schmidt. She will be reading during Poetry International at the South Bank in the autumn and *The Dream of the Unified Field* will be reviewed by Mark Doty in the next issue.

Back home, the biggest prize going, the £30,000 Orange Award for women's fiction has been won by Helen Dunmore for her novel *A Spell of Winter*.

Her new novel *Talking to the Dead* was published in May. She joins the exclusive club of the genuine poet/novelists.

The Faber Memorial Prize has been won by Kathleen Jamie for *The Queen of Sheba*. The prize is given alternately for poetry and fiction and Kathleen is the first woman to win the Poetry category – make of that what you will. This year's judges were all men: William Scammell, Sean O'Brien and Adam Thorpe.

At The Society of Authors, Katherine Pierpoint won a £5000 Somerset Maugham award (she is also *Sunday Times* Young Writer of the Year – another £5000). The Gregories (£4000 each) went to Sue Butler, Cathy Cullis, Jane Griffiths, Jane Holland, Chris Jones, Sinead Morrisey, and Kate Thomas. Elizabeth Bartlett, Dorothy Nimmo, Peter Scupham, and Iain Crichton Smith won £2000 Cholmondeley awards.

NETVERSE

Internet newsgroups ought to be great for poetry workshops. Unlike postal workshops, your fellow poets can see your work and respond within hours. Unlike face to face groups, your critics will have had time to digest your offerings. From the other side of the fence, you don't have to try to think of something to say about everything. It really ought to work. But it doesn't.

The most popular poetry group is **rec. arts.poems**, which sees a lot of activity. Most of this consist of truly abysmal verse; most of the rest is mudslinging. There are less hectic groups: **alt.lesbian.feminst.poetry** occasionally has interesting stuff, though it's on continuous red alert against homophobic air-raids. **christnet.poetry** is safer but it suffers from terminal doggerel syndrome. Possibly the best is **alt.language.urdu. poetry**, but it's a minority interest.

The worthwhile workshops are within commercial networks, rather than on the Internet itself. One of the best is CompuServe. Here you can expect detailed comments on decent poetry. It tends mildly to the nannyish: no Rude Words, no ad hominem comments, and it's dominated by Americans. But there's something going for a place where you can post a poem and within a day or two have comments from California, Canada, Holland, and Brazil.

Oh yes, WWW sites. Well, speaking of Urdu, try **http://www.msci.memphis.edu/~ramamurt/**

ghazal.html for more than you ever wanted to know about ghazals, or **http://www.faximum. com/AHA!POETRY** for an entertaining pot pourri of mainly Japanese forms. Since we have embarked on this multicultural tour, you might like to drop in at **http://www/efn.org/~valdas/ poetry.html** to see how many Lithuanian poets there are. Carry on to some discussion of Turkish poetry with examples and translations at the comprehensive **http://www.cs.umd.edu/users/ sibel/poetry/poetry.html** or sample the exotic Afghan poetry at **http:/www.gl.umbc.edu/~ hqurba1/.Lit/Poems/poems.html**

Let me know of any good sightings, or topics you'd like covered via peter@hphoward.demon. co.uk.

– Peter Howard

NO MORE POEMS (ED.)

The *Spectator*, which had been poem-friendly for some time thanks to P. J. Kavanagh, poetry editor as well as columnist for the magazine, will not be accepting any more poems. The magazine has recently lost much of its always over-inflated allure. This will surely be the final nail in the coffin.

COMPETITION

REPORT ON NO. 1: ADVICE TO POETS

You were asked for pithy advice to poets along the lines of Harry Clifton's "he should twang his guitar in the woodshed a bit more" (John Fuller).

Practical Criticism (Too Late Alas)

If he'd written like Angela Brazil
And less like a gloomy old fart,
He'd have written less piss, he'd have written like
                                        this
And dwelt in the National Heart.

They buck you up, your dads and mums
By golly how they jolly do!
For dads and mums are triffic chums
And mums are angels too!

John Whitworth

Gee Up!
(Tessa Rose Chester)

I could wish before all that dilly-dalliance down
Missenden Way, shedding breakages, confluences,
transparencies and other negatives in her wake so
that one wondered if she would end up like
Humpty Dumpty, that she had traded in her old
grey mare for a sprinter.

    Taken at a gallop the same ground might have
been covered less laboriously in several less sonnets.

    Bearing in my mind that frequent repetition
becomes a drag, Tessa should heed her own advice:
"If it's a question of leaving, just go".

Jessie Smith

The winners receive a selection of current books,
this time including Edna Longley, *Louis MacNeice:
A Study*; Stephen Coote, *John Keats: A Life*; John
Betjeman, *In Praise of Churches*.

NO 2: HOMAGE TO CLICHÉS
See the passage from *Little Dorrit* cited on page 7
of this issue. New elaborated illustrations of worn-
out phrases, in the same manner as the Dickens,
required. They can be either prose or verse. The
phrase itself must not be stated, nor should it
appear on the entry. **Deadline September 1.**

LETTERS

SENTIMENTAL BALLOCKS
Dear Peter,

    I read 'How the Century Lost its Poetry' with
astonishment. For a start it *equates* Eliot with diffi-
culty as though that was all he was about – his point
there is that poetry should be allowed to tackle
difficult subjects and tackling them will inevitably
make it difficult, at least some of the time. This is
an idea that seems to have been mostly lost. Much
of contemporary poetry is so accessible it hardly
needed saying and what amazes me is that you
write as though your side is losing, whereas it's
surely the poets who want the right to be a bit diffi-
cult now and then who tend to get ignored. But
where, if not in poetry, can writers take on complex

issues that involve emotions as well as thoughts?
Poets in the past (Chaucer, Shakespeare, Milton,
Wordsworth, Tennyson) were concerned with the
philosophical problems of their age (Auden, inci-
dentally, more than most). The generation of
Lowell, Berryman and Bishop in the US was still
claiming the right to use poetry to tackle hard
subjects. Our own period is unique in having so
many poets who poohpooh the most important
contemporary thought, to the extent of sounding
like Alan Partridge menaced by French sophistica-
tion. And it doesn't help when they have an influ-
ential ringleader like you in this respect.

    You have an extremely narrow conception of
what postmodernism is: if it involved the attenua-
tion of metaphor no-one could be in favour of it.
Modernist subversion of realism involved the
deployment of metaphor as one of its crucial
devices – *The Waste Land* is constructed around
the key metaphor of fertility. Postmodernism in
many respects develops modernist assumptions
further and usually in a less pained form and
consistently deploys metaphor: magic realism, one
of its key modes, depends on the metaphorical
reading of fantastical imagery. Rushdie's
Midnight's Children and Carter's *Nights at the
Circus* use magic realism partly in order to expose
the extent to which realism is based on Western
and masculine assumptions.

    Incidentally: changing *Schindler's Ark* to
Schindler's List is a shift from metaphor to
metonymy – it's a concession to people who can
only think in a ploddingly realist fashion.

    Then you say that Auden "may be difficult but
not in a modernist way". What does that mean?
What Auden does is to mingle modernism and
realism in a characteristically British hybrid – some
of the best contemporary poets (Fenton, Muldoon,
Duffy, Shapcott) similarly mingle postmodernism
and realism in poetry that is accessible and difficult
by turns. In other words they have flexible, ques-
tioning techniques that allow them to explore
complex issues and make them as comprehensible
as they can. What's the point of diluting poetry
when its audience is always going to be small
compared with that of the Beatles whose words,
apart from the occasional line, were worthless? The
songs you mention were sentimental ballocks.
Sincerely,
IAN GREGSON
Bangor

POUNDING THE BEAT

Dear Peter Forbes,

Behind the journalese of your Editorial, 'How the Century Lost Its Poetry', lies a discomforting ignorance of the history of twentieth century poetry.

You allege that Pound "urged fragmentation of metre", adding that for him, "Modern verse was going to be free verse". This is untrue. What he did urge, in 1912, was for poets "to compose in the sequence of the musical phrase, not in sequence of a metronome" – not the same thing at all.

You also seem to be unaware that as early as 1918, both Eliot and Pound decided that so called "free verse" had gone too far at the hands of their followers, and that a return to fixed metre and rhyme was needed. The fruits of this agreement between the two poets were Pound's *Hugh Selwyn Mauberley* and Eliot's *Poems 1920*, both collections written in regular rhymed stanzas.

As Eliot said, "No *vers* is *libre* for the man who wants to do a good job". Neither Pound nor Eliot believed in the existence of totally free verse. What they did strive for, and memorably achieved in their finest work, was, as Eliot put it, "the inexplicable line with the music which can never be recaptured in other words".

Yours sincerely,
WILLIAM COOKSON
Agenda, London

VICTORIAN VALUES

Dear Editor,

I read with great interest the excellent 'How the Century Lost its Poetry' (*PR* Vol 86 No 1), but remained puzzled by the vehemence with which you reject "Victorian portentousness, ethereality and rhetorical redundancy". Is it the Victorian use or the qualities themselves which are the problem?

Portentous=ominous / awe / extraordinary etc.;
ethereality=light / impalpable / spirit-like;
rhetorical redundancy=aiming to persuade by means of excess / exuberance.

These are qualities which can hardly be thought of as antithetical to poetry of any age, surely? In opposition would be ordinary/insignificant; earthy/down-to-earth/sensual; dispassionate/economic/low-key.

Similarly the "aswoon", from which we were rescued by Eliot's "smell of steaks in passageways"

(used to poor effect in the weak poem offered here as exemplar), means "altered consciousness/faint/sleep" etc., and it's not clear to me why this state should be out of order for poets – though we might want another word for it.

The qualities dismissed here have characterised poetry in all epochs – our own too. Given poets today must compete with journalism, media-scripting and other verbal entertainments, which must make creative and startling use of language, those very qualities might offer poetry its last remaining special role.

The nihilism, cynicism, dispassion generated by our terrifying century, which Eliot and others have captured in poetry, does not exhaust the potential of human consciousness. And the nineteenth century choices made by those in the favourite-poem survey might suggest that other states of mind are valued in poetry.

Whatever the case, the "modern" stance isn't here forever, written in the sky as the only genuine response to the world. It's changing already, and those disapproved states of mind may rise again to open up a new age in poetry.

Yours sincerely,
JUDY GAHAGAN
London

MORE LIGHT ON CANDLES

Dear Peter,

May I have a few words of response to Sheenagh Pugh's letter on the subject of my review of *My Alexandria*.

For the writer, solutions to problems of reanimating tired & deadened language lie in effecting new transfers of meaning for expressive effect, but the fashioning of images can become as much of a knee-jerk reaction to problems of diction as the use of cliché is its thoughtless antithesis. This was at the core of my problem with Mark Doty's book. The use of metaphor as mere ornament is mere linguistic flashiness, it doesn't capture the essence of what is seen, felt or heard. It doesn't in G. M. Hopkins's word, seize the *inscape* of a thing. The MacNeice image of bubbles in the football pools going flat, which Sheenagh Pugh approvingly quotes doesn't work for me. There are no bubbles in football pools. My sympathies go out to the "dull group" she was teaching who made the same objection.

I quoted a line from Doty's poem 'No', objecting to the image "I think the children smell unopened / like unlit candles" because I've never head anybody say: "Open the children will you?" I suppose if you took the word "unopened" out, suggesting the children smelt like unlit candles (a tallow shop?) the image might work, tho I'm not convinced. I cd imagine someone saying "open the candles" (meaning open the packet) so I suppose, if pushed, I cd imagine the children were in packets (openable) or resembled candles (lightable) or even entertain the idea that all three ideas were simultaneously intended (metaphorical hyperaesthesia). But the effect makes me wince.

This image reminded Ms Pugh of Cavafy's poem 'Candles'. That poem derives part of its power, I think, from the fact that one associates massed banks of burning candles with a church. In the poem, however, there's no reference to religion whatsoever. The symbolism of Cavafy's candles is both abundant & bare. He manages to be both profuse & simple at the same time; producing delicate modulations of tone which successfully survive translation. By contrast, Doty has no tone. (Try to imagine translating the poem 'No' into a foreign language.) To compensate for this no tone, Doty drags God into his poem, the phrase "show his face" occurs, & the wood turtle metamorphoses into a "prayer" at the end. I daresay also that image of the children smelling unopened seemed rather clever to him when he wrote it, very complicated and multi-directional but it communicates nothing to me except confusion. (And I don't much care, either, for the way the title of Doty's book tries to appropriate Cavafy's territory: *My* Alexandria. There's something childishly proprietorial about the use of that possessive pronoun.)

Sheenagh Pugh says this book is full of the emotion which she's unable to find in modern British poetry. That strikes me as bizarre. The idea that reading Chaucer or Rilke or Sorley MacLean or Mark Doty would "make me cry" is such a behaviouristic concept of the emotional effect poems have, I can only shrug my shoulders in response. Perhaps there's a curious collusion going on here between writer & reader. One of the poems in Doty's book is called 'Brilliance'. It's about a dying AIDS sufferer. At the end of the poem Doty speculates that in Buddhist reincarnation fashion the subject becomes a goldfish "Fanning the veined translucence / of an opulent tail, / undulant in some capturable curve, / is he bronze chrysanthemums, / copper leaf, hurried darting, / doubloons, icon-colored fins / troubling the water?" This is manipulative (& bad) writing. It tries to cast a spuriously romantic glow over the facts of untimely death & as the initial situation & character of the dying man have been been clearly presented it comes as an intrusion. The would-be "richness" of the diction is a fake. As a reader I feel I've been used.

Sheenagh Pugh, of course, is absolutely entitled to her view of Doty's book. However, exhorting readers to go out and spend seven pounds on it doesn't come across to me as either criticism or enthusiasm but more a kind of self-advertisement: "Don't be dull – for seven quid you can be like me. Look. Poetry makes me cry". It's a great problem at the moment for the state of the art of poetry that there aren't many clear voices around talking plain sense from a clearly defined standpoint. Doty is not without some modest literary skill. He's good at pastiche, for example & T. S. Eliot, of course, was the great master of pastiche, so it seems appropriate that Doty's book shd have won the T. S. Eliot prize. But there's literary skill & there's fraud. It's depressing to see how when the two are combined in the same person everyone is deeply impressed.

Yours sincerely,

JOHN HARTLEY WILLIAMS

Berlin